Whispering in the Wind Endorse

This book is a master class in poetry, teaching writing, and joy. *Whispering in the Wind* provides compelling evidence of what is within reach for all writers. It is a vision you simply cannot walk away from: this book will change you. It is not just the commitment to sketching and watercolor and the beauty of language that her students demonstrate—it is how their essays and reflections show scholarship, curiosity, and wonder. Linda Rief suggests that Heart Books make use of the transitions throughout the school year—all of those brief moments when we are between. Every page in this book sheds light on what is possible in that space.

> PENNY KITTLE, AUTHOR OF *BOOK LOVE, WRITE BESIDE THEM,* AND *180 DAYS*

Linda has been a trusted mentor to me for years. Her respect for teachers is her defining characteristic. In this time of book banning and misinformation, we need poetry more than ever. Her respectful vision for how we can use poems is an essential balm. This book is a blueprint for guiding students in their relationships with poetry forevermore. This feels less like an educator book and more like a companion that shepherds teachers to consider and incorporate the textured versatility of poetry in the classroom and in their lives. We are so lucky to have Linda's words.

> NAWAL QAROONI, EDUCATOR AND AUTHOR

Whispering in the Wind is an excellent resource to help lead your students to discover the joy and beauty of poetry. Through the creation of Heart Books and other engaging strategies, Linda Rief taps into student creativity to ignite their authentic interest in both reading and writing poetry. I love this book. Rief's ideas are fresh, creative, and serve to transform students' negative attitudes about poetry into a lifelong appreciation for the art of verse.

> KELLY GALLAGHER, AUTHOR OF *4 ESSENTIAL STUDIES* AND *180 DAYS*

I've been sharing accessible poems at the beginning of every class meeting for more than thirty years. My students get a good taste of poetry in these daily poetic appetizers. In *Whispering in the Wind*, Linda Rief shows you how to prepare a poetic feast for students. Her ideas, strategies, and recommendations will enhance the literate culture of your classroom.

> Tom Romano, author of *Write What Matters*

Linda Rief's *Whispering in the Wind* feels like an exquisite poem. As I read the beautiful words of Linda and her students, and gaze at their gorgeous Heart Books, I am inspired to expand my own Heart Map. Her book is the antidote to how poetry is often taught in middle school—put through the wringer as we question, scrutinize, and demand answers from poems. Instead, through the process of creating Heart Books, Linda creates space for students to fall in love with poems that reflect the truth of their feelings and the feelings of others. This is a must-have book for all of us who want to engage students in a powerful and authentic reading and writing experience.

> Georgia Heard, author of *Heart Maps* and *Awakening the Heart*

LINDA RIEF

Whispering in the Wind

A Guide to Deeper Reading and Writing Through Poetry

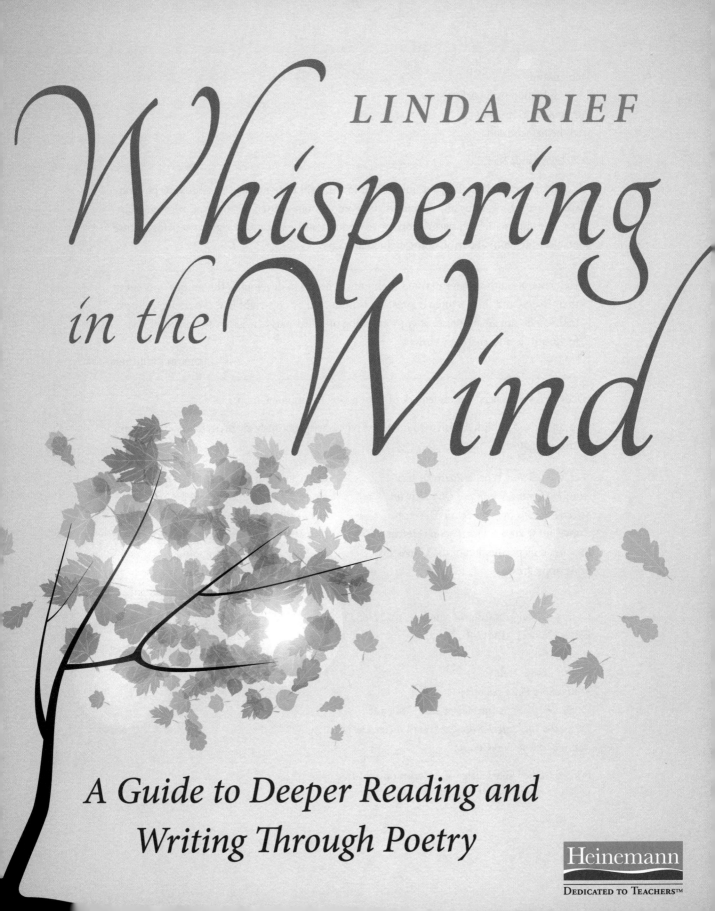

Heinemann

DEDICATED TO TEACHERS™

Heinemann
145 Maplewood Avenue, Suite 300
Portsmouth, NH 03801
www.heinemann.com

The author and publisher wish to thank those who have generously given permission to reprint borrowed material:

"Let Me Tell You What a Poem Brings" from *Half of the World in Light: New and Selected Poems* by Juan Felipe Herrera. Copyright © 2008 by Juan Felipe Herrera. Reprinted by permission of the University of Arizona Press.

Excerpts from blog entry "No more apologies" by Amy Clark, posted August 30, 2017 on *Sometimes You Just Need a Poem*: https://sometimesyoujustneedapoem.blog/2017/08/30/no-more-apologies/. Used by permission of the author.

credits continue on page 199

Library of Congress Control Number: 2022936020
ISBN: 978-0-325-13417-8

Editor: Louisa Irele
Production: Patty Adams
Cover design: Suzanne Heiser and Vita Lane
Typesetter and interior design: Gina Poirier Design
Manufacturing: Val Cooper

Printed in the United States of America on acid-free paper
1 2 3 4 5 VP 26 25 24 23 22   PO# 34007

Contents

PROLOGUE

Finding a Title in the Words of One of My Eighth Graders

After doing Heart Books, I invited my students to reflect on the impact poetry has had on them. So many students admitted unexpected, positive reactions. I was really pleased to see how much poetry had changed them. So many students had such unique ways of metaphorically explaining what they noticed and what they learned. But the words of one student in particular, Domi, took my breath away:

> **Poetry is what whispers in the wind, only to the people that want to hear it. Poetry is like music, it floats and lingers in the air. Poetry lives in waterfalls, falling beautiful and cleansing. It lives within all of us, we just have to find it.**

Domi's words lingered in my mind, the way a good title should. She understood the metaphorical and visual nature of poetry, the "brevity and intentionality" (Clark 2017) of it, and its effect on her, the reader. Forty years in the classroom and I am still learning from my students. Poetry is what "whispers in the wind," guiding us—sometimes knowingly, sometimes unknowingly—toward deeper reading and a heightened awareness of what makes compelling writing.

Whispering in the Wind—that's the title of this book, I thought. Domi has captured all that I had hoped the reading of poetry would do for these eighth-grade readers and writers.

"Poetry may just be the best writing teacher we can offer our students" (Clark 2017). We just have to let students find those poems that *whisper in the wind* all around them and within them.

Let Me Tell You What a Poem Brings
by *Juan Felipe Herrera*

for Charles Fishman
Before you go further,
let me tell you what a poem brings,
first, you must know the secret, there is no poem
to speak of, it is a way to attain a life without boundaries,
yes, it is that easy, a poem, imagine me telling you this,
instead of going day by day against the razors, well,
the judgments, all the tick-tock bronze, a leather jacket
sizing you up, the fashion mall, for example, from
the outside you think you are being entertained,
when you enter, things change, you get caught by surprise,
your mouth goes sour, you get thirsty, your legs grow cold
standing still in the middle of a storm, a poem, of course,
is always open for business too, except, as you can see,
it isn't exactly business that pulls your spirit into
the alarming waters, there you can bathe, you can play,
you can even join in on the gossip—the mist, that is,
the mist becomes central to your existence.

Why Poetry?

As teachers, we might have the wrong idea about what it means to "teach" poetry. . . . So many of us see poetry only as a means to teach figurative language and analytical skills to students, . . . and as a means for students to read the poems that *we* love or that *we* were taught . . . In "schoolifying" poetry, and in only presenting it in this way, we deprive our kids of the opportunity to find themselves in the poems. We deprive them of the opportunity to linger in "the mist" that "becomes central to [their] existence" [Herrera 2008]. And we discount a genre that in its brevity and intentionality is perhaps one of the best writing teachers out there.

—AMY CLARK, 2017

Growing up I never liked poetry. I shuddered each time I heard the word in school. *Poetry* meant finding the hidden meanings the poet had worked so meticulously to hide from his reader. Every word was a symbol for something deep and mysterious, and our task was to unravel all the tricky nuances. I was not good at that. I rejected the entire notion of poetry with the same distaste I had for canned peas or raw oysters. I left the reading and understanding of it to the intellectuals of the world. The smart kids. I was not clever enough to understand it, nor did I like it. Poetry made me feel stupid, and that is not a good feeling. Best to simply avoid it.

Then, years later, I heard William Stafford share his poetry aloud at a reading at Phillips Exeter Academy in Exeter, New Hampshire. I went to the reading reluctantly, only because a former student invited me. Stafford didn't read his poems—he spoke them. He delivered his poetry, simple but eloquent words, riding on his voice and cupped in his hands as if saying, *Here, peek in, look what I noticed that I want you to notice. Feel what I felt at that moment. Taste these words in your mouth and feel how they slip right through to your heart.*

I don't remember a single poem—I just remember his voice, his words, hanging in the air, waiting for me to grab them, to make them mine.

I was astonished. The hour and a half slid away and I was left sitting in the row of chairs emptying as other listeners left. What had just happened? That was *poetry*? I not only understood his words, I loved his words. I loved his voice. He made me feel like his words were mine. He *gave* them to me. His voice said, *Here, take these words. Make them yours.* And I did.

I bought several of Stafford's poetry collections. I began reading poems to myself—the way he read them—as if he was just sharing his thinking with anyone who would listen. I asked my good friend Maureen Barbieri if she knew of any other poets I might like. Did she ever: Mary Oliver, Linda Pastan, Ted Kooser, Nikki Giovanni, Pablo Neruda, Jane Kenyon, Billy Collins, Langston Hughes, Georgia Heard, Naomi Shihab Nye, Galway Kinnell, Richard Wilbur, and on and on. For any occasion at which we exchanged gifts, Maureen's gift to me was always a poetry collection. My shelves are filled with contemporary and classic poets, at home and at school.

I asked my students if they had any favorite poets. Their reaction was my reaction forty years earlier. They cringed at the word *poetry*. Their faces actually changed—eyes widened, shoulders folded, and they pulled into themselves as if protecting their bodies from something horrible.

"No, no," I said. "I heard a poet last night and it was wonderful. I could have listened to him for hours."

They were not convinced. Furthermore, they convinced me why they hated it. Quizzes and tests. Count the syllables. Name the kind of poem it is. Identify the rhyme scheme. Define meter. Write a sonnet. Search for the symbolism. Memorize and present a Robert Frost poem. What's the meaning of the last line . . . the first line . . . every line . . . in his poem "Stopping by Woods on a Snowy Evening"?

I was beginning to hate poetry again just listening to these eighth graders. "Please, please, we're not going to do a *poetry unit*, are we? Say no!" they begged.

And I didn't—do a poetry unit. And I haven't—done a poetry unit.

The irony is, I share lots of poetry with my students as mentor texts from which I ask them to do a quickwrite. My approach to using poetry in this way is deliberate and intentional: share poems on a daily basis in a natural way that allows and encourages a personal response, not an analysis. Students know these mentor texts are often poems, but they are willing to go with me, perhaps because of the trust and rapport I continually try to build with them by inviting them to "write from this poem, anything it brings to mind for you, or borrow any line and write off that line—follow that line, wherever it leads you."

Even when we go back to the poem to look at line breaks or wording or repetition or the use of metaphor or titles, or beginning lines or ending lines, *they seldom make the connection that this is poetry the way they are used to it*—poetry units, quizzes, tests, and hidden meanings. And that's good. They don't reject this poetry, yet . . .

Yet, few of the students, if any, sought out poetry to read on their own. I filled the room with poetry books. I set up a bench with shelves and crates—overflowing with the poetry of both classic and contemporary poets. I tossed in a few poetry anthologies as I book-talked novels. I set the poetry bench up right inside the door to the classroom, so kids had to pass by these books both on their way in and on their way out. Every time a student told me they had forgotten to bring the book they were currently reading for the ten minutes of reading at the beginning of class (Wednesday, Thursday, and Friday), I handed them a book of poetry. And here is the *yet* again: nothing I was doing sent them to this bench on their own for poetry.

I couldn't find the words to explain how I knew or felt that poetry did something that other writing didn't do in the same way. It bothered me that these kids were missing something important because I hadn't found a way to make them seek it out. But I was determined not to further kill their interest in already preconceived notions of poetry by doing a poetry *unit*.

And then, as often happens on the internet, I was searching for something that may or may not have been related to poetry and ended up in that rabbit hole of connections. I stumbled on Mark Doty's lecture on a poetry site about why poetry matters. I read page after page. It was his two last paragraphs that said to me, *Isn't this what you've been looking for?*

> Poetry's work is to make people real to us through the agency of the voice. "Poetry is the human voice," I tell them, "and we are of interest to one another. Are we not?" When people are real to you, you can't fly a plane into the office building where they work, you can't bulldoze the refugee camp where they live, you can't cluster-bomb their homes and streets. We only do those things when we understand people as part of a category: infidel, insurgent, enemy. Meanwhile, poetry does what it does, inscribing individual presence, making a system of words and sounds to mark the place where one human being stood, bound in time, reporting on what it is to be one. In the age of the collective of mass culture and mass market, there's hope in that. . . .
>
> May poetry indeed be a language for a new century. A way to place value on the dignity, specificity, and beauty of individual lives. A way to resist the streamlining diminishment of categories and generalizations. A way to speak, a way to be heard. (Doty 2010)

Indeed, that was what I was looking for. Poetry has the power to make us see and hear each other—one human being at a time. "Poetry is the human voice." I wanted my kids to hear those voices and know each other.

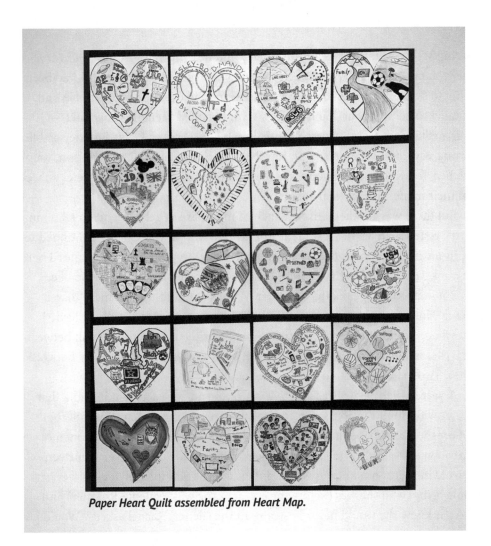

Paper Heart Quilt assembled from Heart Map.

And then—as I approached my classroom from the hallway one day and really looked at the Heart Maps (Heard 1999) the students had created as a means for finding ideas for writing—I stopped and stared. I had organized their Heart Maps into a paper quilt (with twenty maps on each quilt) on the wall outside my door. The intent of posting all of their maps was meant to help students get to know each other and perhaps find writing ideas in other students' Heart Maps, as well as their own. Those things that matter to each of us: people, experiences, songs, books, issues, places—our stories—reside in our hearts.

By crafting the Heart Maps, I wasn't asking kids to write poetry. I was asking them to find the topics that mattered to them for any kind of writing, knowing that if the topic or issue is important to them, the students work hard to make the writing compelling and meaningful to others. Some of them were choosing to write poetry but *few of them were reading poetry*.

As I stood there I thought, *Why have I used these Heart Maps only to inspire writing? What if we used these to inspire reading—the reading of poetry?* Ever since hearing William Stafford "read" his poetry and hearing Ted Kooser (1985) say that "you must read 200 poems before you even begin to write them," I had been trying to figure out a way to get my students to read even more poetry beyond the quickwrites, without doing a *poetry unit*. I wanted them to know poets— William Stafford, Mary Oliver, Naomi Shihab Nye, Andrea Davis Pinkney, Pablo Neruda, Kwame Alexander, Sarah Kay, Nikki Grimes, Jacqueline Woodson, Ralph Fletcher, Ted Kooser—the same way they know musical groups or athletes so well that their names roll off their tongue.

But there was another reason. Much of my desire to get students to read more poetry rested with Savitri, a student from India, whose whole being continued to live in my heart, even years after having her in eighth grade. When I handed her the book *This Same Sky* (Nye 1992), I hoped she would find a poem she liked, a poem that would speak directly to her. What she found was far more than a poem. "Home" by Nasima Aziz, an Indian poet, spoke so personally to Savitri that when she chose to read the poem aloud, a bridge was not only built between the writer and his reader, but also built between this young woman and her class-mates. Two bridges that told her she was not alone in her longing.

A year earlier, Savitri was severely injured in an auto accident in India that left her with double vision, an uncontrollable tremor in one hand, a right foot that dragged heavily behind her as she walked, and limited short-term memory. Savitri longed to be "normal." When she read aloud the poem, every fourteen-year-old in that room knew it wasn't only India she was longing for—it was her whole being, who she was (before the accident she was a talented runner) and who she knew she would never be again. In the silence, Rachel asked, "Would you read that again?"

With the voice, the timing, and the confidence of a poet, Savitri breathed life into Aziz's words. In the spontaneous burst of applause that followed her reading, she smiled. In their lives, those students may never hear a more beautiful, pas-sionate, or powerful reading of a poem. The breathtaking words of a poet from India, translated scrupulously in a collection by Naomi Shihab Nye, published by a perceptive editor in a skyscraper in New York, touched a child's life. An entire classroom of peers understood in that moment a bit of what her life was like and how painful her longing was.

I want kids to develop an understanding of others' feelings, a compassion that says *I know you. I know what you are feeling*. That's what I want all students to find in poetry—the truth of their feelings and the feelings of others. Rudine Sims Bishop (1990) clarifies this when she says that books act as windows, mirrors, and sliding glass doors.

> Books are sometimes windows, offering views of worlds that may be real or imagined, familiar or strange. These windows are also sliding glass doors, and readers have only to walk through in imagination to become part of whatever world has been created and recreated by the author. When lighting conditions are just right, however, a window can also be a mirror. Literature transforms human experience and reflects it back to us, and in that reflection we can see our own lives and experiences as part of the larger human experience. Reading, then, becomes a means of self-affirmation, and readers often seek their mirrors in books. (ix)

Students not only find connections to themselves in poetry, but an understanding of others. When I set up the Heart Books, I originally thought kids would find predominantly the poetry that connected personally to them. What they showed me is that they found poetry that let them see people and places outside of their own experiences. Poets showed them their lives, their beliefs, their feelings—that my students may never have experienced. Poetry opened *their* world but led them through the door to *the world of others*.

Touched by the Heart Map idea of Georgia Heard, inspired by the writing and speaking of William Stafford and Mark Doty, believing the words of Ted Kooser, and humbled by the voice and courage of Savitri, I embarked on the idea of Heart Books to inspire and deepen the reading—and ultimately the love—of poetry.

Heart Maps as Inspiration for Reading Poetry

The Heart Maps would become the covers of blank books, and the impetus for finding poems connected to all those things that mattered the most to the students. I wanted them to do more than simply collect poems. I wanted them to spend time with them: read them (maybe several times), think about them, write, draw, or sketch a response to them. Jot down why they chose the poem. What they noticed or thought about it. What in the poem made them think that? What did they notice about the way it was written? How did the way it was written deepen or change the way it was read? What did the poet have to say about writing, about reading, about poetry?

I wanted my students to feel what I felt listening to William Stafford—to feel something in a way that makes them hold their breath. Stop time. See, hear, and feel ordinary things in extraordinary ways. Recognize how words and formats are used in refreshing, surprising ways. See the world and their lives poetically. Live in the words of poets that touched their hearts. Find classic and contemporary poets to love and emulate. Use their artistic strengths and imaginations to illustrate the poems that spoke to them. Get their creative juices flowing. Learn how poets use reading and writing in their own lives. Sit beside a poem long enough to experience the richness of its words, the intensity of its feeling; sit beside a poem long enough to wonder, *How'd the poet do that?*, especially in a way that would help them become stronger writers. What do they notice about the way the poem is written? What craft moves does the poet make, and how do those moves affect the poem and affect the reader?

In the book *Leading from Within* (Intrator and Scribner 2007, 222), the editors suggest asking specific questions that invite engagement with a poem that are precisely the ways I would like my students to engage with their choices of poems:

- What do you notice in this poem?

- Where does this poem intersect with your life?

- What initially attracted you to this poem?

- What is happening in this poem and to whom?

- What do you find elusive or opaque?

  - With my students I might rephrase this to:

    What confuses you?

    What do you find problematic about this poem?

- What do you sense the poem is trying to tell you?

- What images, words, or phrases seem to linger in your mind?

- Who would you give this poem to and why?

Some students might need the specificity of the questions as they approach their reading of poetry in this open-ended way. All the questions are only meant to guide them in their ability to enter deeply into their reading and thinking.

Poetry as Inspiration for Robust Reading and Heightened Quality of Writing

Ultimately, I want the students to notice the poetry in anything they read—novels, editorials, informational pieces, articles—anything. I want the students to realize that sitting beside clear, beautiful language, steeped in strong feelings, could enrich and elevate their own writing in any genre.

In the author's notes at the end of *Pachinko*, Min Jin Lee (2017) describes how reading poetry and recognizing the verse in prose became a pivotal part of her writing process. She began to see the "music in sentences and paragraphs," and she wondered how the author took her into new worlds and made her feel things so strongly. She also "read every fine novel and short story I could find, and I studied the ones that were truly exceptional. If I saw a beautifully wrought paragraph, say from Julia Glass's *Three Junes*, I would transcribe it in a marble notebook. Then, I would sit and read her elegant sentences, seemingly pinned to my flimsy notebook like a rare butterfly on cheap muslin. Craft strengthened the feelings and thoughts of the writer." (Lee 2017, 508)

It is this crafting of phrases and sentences that I want my students to notice in any of their reading. I began to think that it might be in the reading of poetry that they might first notice that tight, purposeful writing that would lead them to see the poetry in all kinds of prose. When I did book talks of recommended books, I used passages such as the following to not only give the students a sense of the style of the writing but also to notice the poetry in the prose.

Read the following passage from *Where the Crawdads Sing* by Delia Owens (2018) and marvel at the poetry of this excerpt:

> A great blue heron is the color of gray mist reflecting in blue water. And like mist, she can fade into the backdrop, all of her disappearing except the concentric circles of her lock-and-load eyes. She is a patient, solitary hunter, standing alone as long as it takes to snatch her prey. Or, eyeing her catch, she will stride forward one slow step at a time, like a predacious bridesmaid. And yet, on rare occasions she hunts on the wing, darting and diving sharply, swordlike beak in the lead. (88)

SECTION ONE: Why Poetry?   9

As I read this novel and copied so much of the metaphorical language into my notebook, I realized her extended metaphors offered the reader deeper connections into all we learned about the main character, Kya. She is the great blue heron.

Or consider this passage from *The Astonishing Color of After* by Emily X. R. Pan (2018):

> When he finally got the words out, his voice crawled through
> an ocean to get to me. It was a cold cerulean sound, far away
> and garbled. . . Where I was that day: on the old tweed couch
> in Axel's basement, brushing against his shoulder, trying
> to ignore the orange wall of electricity between us.
> If I pressed my mouth to his, what would happen?
> Would it shock me like a dog collar? (2)

Falling in love but not wanting to believe it. What's it like? An "orange wall of electricity," shocking, "like a dog collar." The metaphors heighten the intensity, and we shake our heads, yes, that's what it was like.

Or this passage from Jason Reynolds' (2016) *Ghost*:

> I squatted down, pushed my feet back against the blocks,
> stretched out my thumbs and index fingers and placed them
> on the edge of the white starting line. Rested my weight on
> my arms. Closed my eyes. Thought of us running to the door.
> Running for our lives.
>
> "Get set!" said the starter. Butts in the air. The sound of the
> gun cocking. The sound of the door unlocking. Heart pounding.
> Breathe. Breathe. Breathe. Silence. This. Is. It.
>
> And then . . . *BOOM!* (180)

These books are novels. But this is poetry. Poetry. The just-right words, their intentional placement, the feeling that comes over me as the pace, the rhythms roll off my tongue—the slow silence of the "patient, solitary hunter, standing alone as long as it takes" or hearing "his voice—a cold, cerulean sound—crawl through an ocean to get to me" or the feeling of my heart pounding, beating louder, faster, like the "gun cocking, the door unlocking, breathe, breathe, breathe." Poetry. This is poetry. The chosen words and their arrangements force me to slow down, to "pay attention, be astonished," says Mary Oliver (2008), as she invites us to really *see* the world.

Read the lead to Michael Christie's (2015) article "All Parents Are Cowards" and marvel at the poetry of his writing.

Read Naomi Shihab Nye's (2008) "Gate A-4" and ask yourself and your students: Anecdote? Personal narrative? Editorial? All of these, and yet, poetry. Poetry.

Owens, Pan, Reynolds, Christie, and Nye make us feel something. They put us in the experience with them. We look up from the page of writing we have just read—and most likely have reread—and think, *That is poetry*. I want to write like that. I want my students to write like that.

Immersed in the reading of all genres, especially poetry, our students may begin to see and understand that the best writing, the strongest writing, is poetry. My greatest hope is that they begin to recognize the strength of poetic language in the crafting of their own writing. Reading as writers. Seamless *transitions* from reading to writing.

Yes, finding ways to get students to read more poetry, to recognize the poetry in any writing, and to believe they, too, could write like this, is definitely worth doing.

Heart Books

Make Poetry Reading a Practice

*T*hen the practicality of this idea kicked in. I have the students for less than fifty minutes each day. What must I leave out to squeeze this in?

Transitions. Of course. I would leave nothing out. I would use all those wasted hours to fill in during those *transition* times between various kinds of reading and writing, or the day or two before a vacation when I don't want to start looking at different genres, or the day or two after vacations to get kids back into the swing of reading and writing, or all those times during and after standardized testing when many students have finished the test and sit waiting for classmates to finish. There are so many transition times in schools, and this would be valuable and practical during these times.

Not just practical, but intellectually important transitions. I want the students to see the poetry in all their reading—the way authors invoke surprising images, intense feelings, and compelling ideas in the way they shape language. Could, and would, students use these discoveries in poetry in their writing in any genre? So many valuable *transitions*.

If I designed and framed the idea carefully, kids could pick up or put down their Heart Books without skipping a beat. (Pun intended.) No matter where they left off, it would be easy to step right back into their thinking. The Heart Books needed only to stay in the room, organized by sections in bins, easy to access on a moment's notice. Poetry books in one place. Art supplies plentiful and accessible in another place. Yes, this could work well. And it does.

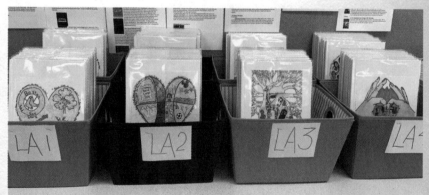

Heart Books: Kept in bins and organized by language arts section for easy access

Creating the Heart Books

FIRST STEPS

This section lays the groundwork for this project, explaining how to build the Heart Books and how to introduce poetry as a genre to the students. First steps take several days, sometimes even a full week, but it's worth the time to get students prepared for working relatively independently for the rest of the year on these Heart Books.

Gather Materials

Before you start, you will need to gather some materials:

◆ One blank book per student: I like to use 8½ × 11-inch blank books from Bare Books but there are many other possible resources. You could even use digital programs like Padlet.

◆ Poetry books or collections: Include both contemporary and classic poets and ensure that poems are about diverse topics from poets of diverse backgrounds.

◆ Art supplies: Construction paper, watercolor paper, paint boxes, brushes, colored pencils, crayons, scissors . . .

Map Your Heart

In our writer's-reader's notebooks, we list those things that matter most to us, those things that "live in our hearts." What memories, moments, people, animals, objects, places, books, fears, scars, friends, siblings, parents, grandparents, journeys, secrets, dreams, songs, relationships, comforts, learning experiences? What's at the center? What's around the edges? What colors represent different emotions, events, or relationships?

Adapted from Georgia Heard's (1999) book *Awakening the Heart*, I give the students the following questions to consider (if they need something more concrete and/or specific). I list these questions on the whiteboard or the computer and leave them up so students can see them as they map their hearts first in their notebooks. This is rough draft planning, sketching, and writing.

- What are some things close to your heart . . . that have stayed in your heart?

- What activities do you love doing? Spend time doing?

- Who and what do you really care about?

- What issues in the world matter to you?

- What people have been important to you?

- What are some experiences or central events that you will never forget?

- What happy or sad memories do you have?

- What small things/objects are important to you—a tree or pond in your backyard, a stuffed animal, a poster, a trophy . . . ?

- What kinds of things do you love to do with friends? Family?

- Where have you been that you love? New York City? The Grand Canyon?

- What scares you? Worries you? Concerns you? Makes you nervous?

- What books and songs do you love?

- What famous quote or saying speaks to who you are?

Make Heart Maps

The next step is for students to create the Heart Maps themselves, using those things that matter most to them. Students begin by drawing or tracing a heart shape onto oak tag or other heavy drawing paper that is precut to fit on the cover of the blank book. They can choose the metaphorical heart shape we see most often on Valentine's Day or a sketch that resembles more closely the anatomical heart, or any design that resembles a heart, such as shaping their hands into a heart. I give kids samples of these heart shapes, easily found on numerous websites like crayola.com or firstpalette.com. I remind students to think artistically as they design their map and "use pencil for your rough draft, just to make sure your drawings and words fit in the heart shape. Use those things that matter to you as listed in your writer's-reader's notebook to draw onto your Heart Map."

In *Awakening the Heart* and in her Ted talk on YouTube, Georgia Heard says that Heart Maps provide "a pathway to clarity" of our stories, our feelings, our experiences. Crafting a Heart Map guides us inward, helping to make our unknowns known so we can "live our lives with compassion and purpose." These maps help kids navigate who they are and what they care about in the world. Reason enough to construct them.

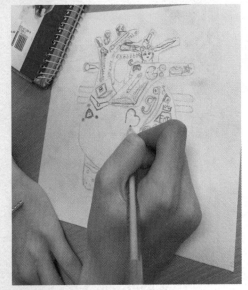

Students designing their Heart Maps

I put examples of a variety of Heart Maps completed in previous years around the room for students to look at. I point out how kids designed their maps, used color, shapes, words, or sketches. Before I had any examples from my students, I

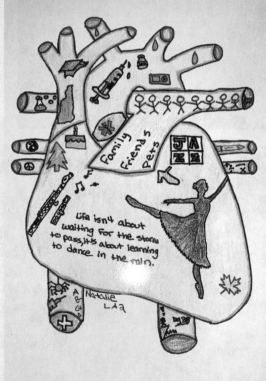

Completed Heart Maps with unique designs

used ones found in Heard's book. There are many examples of completed Heart Maps in this book that you're welcome to show your students until you have enough examples of your own.

Some Heart Maps show real creativity in design and include so many of the things important to each student through words and visuals. Students were thoughtful and thorough in the planning and crafting of each map.

Mount your students' maps on the classroom wall as a quilt or on a bulletin board. The completed Heart Maps provide a great opportunity for students to get to know each other in the same way they do by reading each other's writing. You could allow students to passively look through their peers' Heart Maps, or you could ask them to do something more specific, such as: "As you browse through your peers' Heart Maps, write down at least three to five things that come to mind for you. Spencer's family tradition is finding and riding as many roller coasters as they can as a family. This makes me think of the fear I have of riding roller coasters and fear of heights. Driving up the narrow, winding road to Mt. Washington, I was white-knuckle terrified we would slip over the cliff.

Natalie's and Kathy's biological hearts make me think of my dad, his heart attack, and how hard our hearts work to keep us alive. These notes in my notebook and notes in their notebooks all cover more possibilities for writing."

You could leave the Heart Maps up for a few days or weeks until students are ready to begin their Heart Books.

Heart Books

Create Heart Books

When it's time to begin the Heart Books, which is any time convenient for you, give each student a blank book. Have the students cut out their Heart Maps and glue them onto the front cover of the blank book.

Next, distribute the Heart Book Instructions (see Appendix) and have students glue them on the first page of the blank book. I *do not read* the instructions to them. Instead, I ask them only to read the three questions at the top of the page:

- What comes to mind when you hear the word *poetry*?

- What makes poetry different from other kinds of writing?

- Who are your favorite poets? What do you like about their poetry?

Because I want to see if doing these Heart Books will really help students find value in reading poetry, I ask them to tell me their thinking before we begin by answering the questions on the *left side* of the first two-page spread. Their perceptions vary from blunt distaste to sophisticated assumptions about the genre. I've included just a small sampling here, but it represents many other students with similar understandings.

Some years I have asked students to first tell me what's on their Heart Map and why it is important to them. The intent is to get them to explain in a bit more depth the *why* of each item that might contribute to their search for a relevant poem and/or help me talk to them about possibilities for writing topics. In some cases, it is helpful; in others, it is just a relisting in words of those items visually represented. What I am most interested in is their thinking about poetry *before* and *after* making their Heart Books.

I tell students to leave the *right side* of this first double-page spread blank for now. After students have spent the year gathering and responding to the poems they've chosen, I ask them to respond on the right-hand side to these same three questions (as listed previously) now that they have read so many more poems. (See pages 152–154 to see what they now think about poetry after doing the Heart Book.)

Students' Thoughts on Poetry *Before* the Heart Books

When I think of poetry I think of boredom and gobbledygook that just expresses how depressing the poet's life is. In poetry you always have to analyze every sentence and it's so boring. I wish they could just tell you instead of writing all fancy Shakespearean stuff that beats around the bush.

I don't follow any poets. Yet. (Sam)

When I hear the word *poetry*, I think of a message or something personal that only the writer fully understands. I think of true feelings spilling out onto paper, but always remaining a mystery or an unsolved puzzle.

Poems are mysterious and should leave you with questions. They should make you wonder and imagine what was happening in the poem. They should make you experience the feeling in the poem. They can be extremely personal without being obvious. Poetry isn't always easy to understand, but it's good to have to think and ponder while reading. If you take a moment to think about the poem you're reading, you can always find a piece of it to relate to.

My favorite poet is Ellen Hopkins, who writes poetry novels, like: *Perfect*, *Impulse*, *Glass*, and *Burn*. Her poems are scary and mysterious and give you strong feelings of anger and sadness. I like that because they are powerful enough to have an impact on me. (Maegan)

Poetry is agony and a waste of time. (Devin)

To be honest, I've never really liked reading or writing poetry. Whenever I hear the word *poetry* I think of metaphoric riddles, similes, and personification. . . . One of the reasons I like poetry is because there is a lot of white space on the page and, therefore, it's quicker to read.

Poetry is different from other kinds of writing in that the poet is allowed to use fragments of sentences and the message isn't as clear as in prose. The readers can have different ideas about what the poem is saying, and they both could be right.

I like Robert Frost because some of the first poems that I read were by him. I like that he is a poet from New Hampshire and that his poem "Nothing Gold Can Stay" was in *The Outsiders*. (Lucas)

Poetry makes me think a jumble of things. If I hear the word in LA class I think of boring assignments and reflections. Anywhere else images of Robert Frost and Odysseus run through my brain. (Nate)

When I hear the word *poetry*, the word itself doesn't come to mind. Instead, I think of color. The deepest purples and brightest yellows, royal blues, and lush greens. A carnival of light and sound explodes in my head. I think of all the poems I've read, all the songs I've heard, all the art work I've seen. Poetry to me is so much more than just a category of writing; it's an art form.

Poetry is different from any other kind of writing. It's musical, personal, unique, and beautiful. Poetry can be enjoyed as so much more than just writing on a page. It is not only seen, but heard, felt, tasted, smelt, and appreciated in every sense. So meaningful and so loved.

I like reading Edgar Allen Poe for his complex and mysterious ways. I enjoy the simplicity and plain humor offered by Shel Silverstein. Robert Frost has nice work as well; it's pleasant to read and wonderful to listen to. (Madison)

When I hear the word *poetry* I think of broken lines, rhymes, and rhythms. I think of Shel Silverstein and Robert Frost. I think of long, boring pieces of writing that are called "epics," as well as short poems that address issues or are just funny.

A lot of times, poetry is about the same sort of subjects that other types of writing are about. The difference is in the packaging. Poetry is more artistic than other types of writing because of its rhythm and rhymes.

I don't know many poets, but my favorite that I have read is Shel Silverstein. Even now, much older than I was when I first read him, his silly poems give me a smile. (Jacob)

Introduce Heart Books: Show Possibilities

After the students have shared their thoughts about poetry, I review the instructions with them.

I believe if something is important enough for students to do, it must be important enough for me to do. Before they begin looking for their first poem, I share my Heart Map and my first double-page spread.

I care deeply about teaching and writing, which is why I chose "The Writer" by Richard Wilbur (1988) for my first poem. I tell my kids why I chose this poem, what it means to me, and why I chose to use photos of students writing to illustrate his words. I read a few of Wilbur's words about poetry, about reading, about writing to them, and then I share my response:

My Heart Map

Don Graves, my first teacher/mentor at the University of New Hampshire in the Master of Arts in Teaching program, gave me "The Writer" in the first course I took as a grad student. He *said* it to us. He knew the poem by heart (knowing something "by heart" implies we own it, we have made it ours in our own way). So, this is a poem, I thought. I don't have to memorize it and no one is going to test me on its meaning. I have come to love this poem for all it says to me about writing. It is hard work. We write what matters to us. And like the starling, sometimes we beat ourselves as we try to find what we want to say and how to say it well. It's persistence— patience—going back to it again and again—before the writing works." Writing is who we are—our voices, our stance, our beliefs, our opinions, our feelings. It is serious work, hard work. It feels good when we do it well and can nudge our own thinking, as well as someone else's. As a teacher I see each student as "the writer," nudging them to go back to it again and again—tough as it is—to write what matters to them in a way that matters to others.

I reiterate to the students that the poem itself is not as important as their response to it. There is no "right" poem that they choose. What matters is why they chose it, what they noticed about it, and what it means to them. There are no "right" answers even to these suggestions. As the year progresses, their choices of poems have more to do with being intrigued by the poem and little to do with their Heart Maps. They are finding poetry that engages them, and if they are taking the poetry to heart, they are finding poetry that *changes* them.

If you have never made your own Heart Map, start yours with your students. Search for a poem, plan out your first double-page spread, and talk through the process to show them how much this matters to you as well.

Before introducing the students to poets and poetry, I show them several double-page spreads from previous years, just so they have a few visual examples of ways students chose to organize their layout of the two pages. I post these examples around the room so that the kids can refer to them. I share these double-page spreads *before* they begin looking for poems so that I am not interrupting their search for poems and their reading of them.

As I show them these examples, I ask: "What do you notice about these pages?" They notice that some students typed their poem and response, while others handwrote. They noticed the illustrations were done in cut paper, watercolor, pencil, or pen drawing, and sometimes the illustration spread across the two pages. They noticed some illustrations were simple, others were complicated, yet they all connected to, or enhanced, the poem. They noticed each student must have "spent time figuring out where to put everything on the two pages." You might use some of my students' pages to ask the same question of your students: What do they notice these students did?

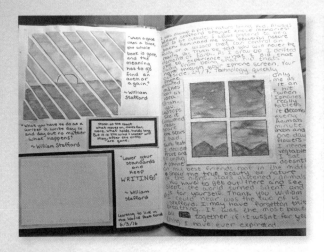

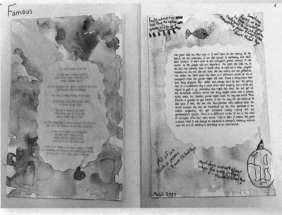

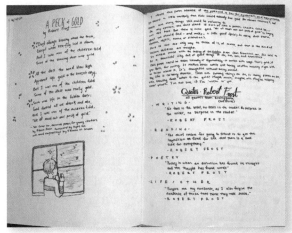

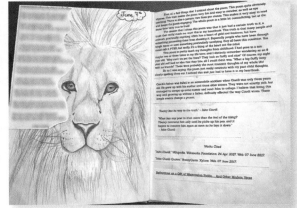

Examples of organization and layout of pages

Introduce Students to Poets and Poetry

"By the time we get to high school, we expect kids to be able to make the leap from having loved Shel Silverstein in third grade to being able to appreciate Shakespeare's Sonnet 73," says Kwame Alexander. "The world doesn't work like that. You've got to have bridges to help kids get from there to here, to cross over, so to speak, so they can appreciate Mary Oliver, Naomi Shihab Nye, and Langston Hughes."

—Boothbay Literacy Retreat June 2016

Choosing Poets and Poems

The poems we choose to put in front of our students, to read to students, to recommend to students, to make available to students, are the bridges that help them navigate the road from Silverstein to Shakespeare. What we choose to share often determines whether they will step onto that bridge or refuse the invitation.

Share Micah Bournés reading Ntozake Shange's poem "My Father Is a Retired Magician" (micahbournes.bandcamp.com "Echoes of the Foremothers"). It will render them speechless and asking, no begging, to hear more poetry.

Few of us have the powerful voice of Bournés, but we can practice reading a poem aloud *before* we read it to the students. We want to show the students we care enough about the poem and them to *know* it: the pronunciation, the punctuation, the pace, and the feeling. It is important for the students to see and hear these poems. I don't remember which poet said, "We should always give a poem twice," but I often give a poem three times, or more.

The first reading is to let the kids hear it and follow along on the text.

During the second reading, I ask the kids to underline any phrases or lines that resonate with them or write the line in their writer's-reader's notebooks if I am showing them the poem from the whiteboard or computer. We then choose one of those lines and do a quickwrite: write for two to three minutes, either anything the poem brings to mind, *or* borrow one of the lines, letting the line lead their thinking.

After the third reading, I ask students: "What do you notice about the poem, either the content or the way it is written?"

I start with Micah Bournés or with Tupac Shakur's "In the Depths of Solitude." I don't tell them it belongs to Tupac just yet. His book *The Rose That Grew from Concrete* is worth buying, but this poem is easily found online at http://allpoetry.com/In-The-Depths-Of-Solitude. I use his handwritten version to show them—you can put copies on their tables or display on a screen. I want to engage the students immediately and take them beyond flowers and stars and rhyming. I want them to see poets beyond Shel Silverstein and Robert Frost.

Not surprisingly, many students recognize Tupac's writing. When I ask of this piece "What do you notice?" they say: "It doesn't rhyme, it doesn't have punctuation, sometimes it uses numbers and letters in place of words, sometimes it uses caps, other times it doesn't . . . that's a poem?! Are you allowed to do that? Is that legal? I like it."

Another poem to begin with is Kwame Alexander's "Awkward Poems" from *Crush* ♥ *Love Poems* (2007, 33–34):

Awkward Poems

Sometimes i wish we weren't friends
then i could gaze into your bold eyes
and find answers to questions i'm afraid to ask
but for now, i'll stick to quick glances
and other friendly gestures

Sometimes i wish we weren't friends
then i could hold your hands in ways
that made your palms moist from suggestion
but for now, i'll stick to high fives
and other friendly gestures

Sometimes i wish we weren't friends
then i could hijack your bronze lips,
take them hostage and steal their suppleness
but for now, i'll stick to light pecks
and other friendly gestures

Continues

Continued

What i am trying to say is
i love
glancing
lingering
flirting
and being your friend

but one day
one day real soon
i'm gonna put away those
big
soft
dark
friendly gestures
and get close
get real close to you

but for now, i'll stick to awkward poems
and other friendly gestures

What do students notice about this poem? It doesn't rhyme; it repeats several phrases, usually three times each; there is only punctuation inside the poem; it uses the lowercase *i* several times; sometimes there is only one word in a line.

Later, when we are talking about craft moves in relation to any writing we are working on, we will go back to these two poems and several others and try to figure out what each of those craft moves does for the poem and for the reader. For instance, what does the lowercase *i* do in Alexander's poem and/or make you think as a reader? Students surmise: he feels small or unimportant around this girl, he has little confidence in himself, he accepts the relationship of just being a "friend," nothing bigger. The *lowercase i* reinforces all of those feelings.

Noticing a craft move is a big step, but being able to articulate what that technique does to the writing and/or the reader shows students how to use craft moves in their own writing. These poems that I use for introductions to poetry for the Heart Books reinforce the value of noticing, naming, and using the craft moves purposefully and intentionally.

We don't need to be the one to find all the poems to share with students. We can, and should, be receptive to their suggestions as it shows we trust them as readers and value their choices. I share a poem from *Light Filters In* by Caroline Kaufman, which was recommended to me by several students.

mercury:

my mood changes
too fast for my brain
to keep up with.

sometimes, I am okay.
I really am.
talking,
working,
laughing.

then suddenly,
day trades places with night
and my neurons freeze.
I stop talking.
I stop working.
I stop laughing.

all I can do
is pray the frostbite
doesn't reach my heart
before the sun rises again.

In my planning of what poems I share with students, in addition to the several I mentioned already, I frequently show and read:

- Kobie Bryant's "Dear Basketball"
- Naomi Shihab Nye's "Boy and Mom at the Nutcracker Ballet" (1998) from Nye's *Fuel*
- Edwin A. Hoey's "Foul Shot" (1966) from *Reflections on a Gift of Watermelon Pickle* [Dunning, Lueders, and Smith 1966]
- Marilyn Nelson's "Cafeteria Food" (2001) from *Carver: A Life in Poems*
- Pablo Neruda's "The Father" or "Shyness" (2010) from Ryan's *The Dreamer*
- Elizabeth Acevedo's "Unhide-able" (2018) from *The Poet X.*

These are nontraditional pieces that hook the kids right away and that, I believe, they are likely to relate to.

My students also love spoken word poetry and video poems. Show it once, then show it again with printed copies of the words in front of them. Invite them to find a line that resonates with them or respond to the poem as a whole. Keeping this thinking in their writer's-reader's notebook lets them capture initial thoughts that often lead to more extensive thinking. (Recommended spoken word poets and video poems are listed in the Appendix.)

One way to hook students is to share a poem or poet that is connected to your community or with whom your students may be familiar. For example, Ralph Fletcher lives in our school district and my students are familiar with his novels, but they don't usually know his poetry. I show them one of Ralph's collection of poems, *Ordinary Things* (1997), and explain how it came to be on a walk that is so familiar to my kids: the loop that circles our middle school and our high school.

I read one of his poems, asking if any of them have seen what Ralph saw on this walk. The students are stunned and fascinated by the fact there is so much poetry in the ordinary, especially ordinary things with which they are so familiar.

I open Abigail Becker's (1993) now-out-of-print collection *A Box of Rain* and tell kids what I know about Abi, who died at age sixteen in a horrific automobile accident, and how this book came to be. I read one of her poems, collected from her journals by her sisters and her mom, who taught sixth grade at our middle school, and published in this collection of Abi's writing and art. These are books I know my students will connect with right away.

As I read a poem from each of these poets, I point out there are hard copies on the tables so kids can see them, as well as hear them.

You know your students, your school, your environment better than anyone. I begin with what I know my students will relate to. You should begin with the poems you know your students can connect to. If you live in the city, perhaps you begin with Allan De Fina's (1997) *When a City Leans Against the Sky*, or Tupac Shakur's (1999) *The Rose That Grew from Concrete*, or Jacqueline Woodson's (2014) *Brown Girl Dreaming*, or Kwame Alexander's (2018a) *Rebound*, or Rupi Kaur's (2015) *Milk and Honey*.

When choosing the poems I share with students, I keep the following questions in mind:

◆ Are the imagery and wording accessible? Are the students able to enter into the poem and understand most of the language? Can they see the imagery in their heads? Can they hear the rhythm and music in the phrasing and word choices?

- Is this poem both personal enough and universal enough to engage and expand the students' perceptions of themselves and the world?

- Is the poem short enough to sustain the students' interest?

- Is it clear enough to understand the point? Is it mysterious enough to raise questions and wonderings?

- Have I intentionally found a variety of culturally diverse voices and perspectives?

If you know your students' experiences with poetry have been limited, start with a poet with whom they are familiar, giving them words and feelings they recognize and understand. Start with poems that are accessible, comfortable—moving them slowly to new poets who will nudge and challenge their thinking.

I do not read all of these poems at once. I spread them out over one or two days a week, every six-to-seven weeks, while we are working on the Heart Books. These are the poets I want the kids to begin to recognize. There are so many others.

When I show and read these poems (often several times), I ask the students to pay attention to some, or all, of the following, in the hopes they will do or notice some of these same things in the poems they choose for themselves:

- **What's a line that stood out to you? In your writer's-reader's notebook, jot down quickly—for two to three minutes—all that the line brought to mind for you, letting the line lead your thinking.**

- **As a whole, what does the poem bring to mind for you?**

- **What do you notice about this poem?**

- **What do you notice specifically about the title, the beginning, the ending, white space, length of lines, use of punctuation, word choices, point of view, perspective, tense, line breaks, how lines end or run together, layout on the page, stanzas, metaphors . . . (*never* all of these at once, just one or two noticeable techniques in a specific poem)?**

- **What is a particular craft move or technique the poet uses in this poem? How does it affect the poem and/or you, the reader?**

Sometimes "hoping" kids notice or pay attention to all (or any) of these things in the poems they choose is not enough. I put a border around these suggestions, so that you might make a copy to share with your students if you think it would be helpful to them. The list is simply a gentle reminder to students of all we talked about in the shared poems that *might* be helpful in their thinking about their chosen poems. What I *don't* want to do is ruin the feeling a reader takes from a poem by asking lots of questions or steering their response in any direction other than their own.

On a bulletin board and/or in a three-ring binder, I post or collect a copy of each poem I read aloud because kids often want to return to those poems to find others by the same poet. I also show them where I have assembled all the art supplies for their use, briefly explaining the variety of tools available. In the Art Invitations (see the Appendix), I list the supplies needed for each technique, but in general I have lots of colored pencils, watercolor sets, paint brushes, scissors, rulers, construction paper, and watercolor paper available.

Let's pause for a moment, take a breath, and review what we've done so far and the order in which we've done it. I cannot tell you how long each of these steps takes, except that I take the time during the first six weeks to somehow fit this in. Keep in mind that most of the work with Heart Books is completed after we've done all that is listed below and during *transition times*—those times in between the writing and reading you do on a regular basis. Everything I've described up to this point is done first, so the students are set to work independently during transition times. The students have done all of the following:

- created a Heart Map

- received a blank book

- glued their Heart Map to the cover of the blank book, which is now called their Heart Book

- received and glued their instructions into their Heart Book

- written what comes to mind when they hear the word *poetry*

- seen what a double-page spread might look like

- read and reviewed the instructions glued in their Heart Book

- seen my Heart Book and heard my response to the first poem I chose

- been introduced to several poems and poets and talked through what they notice in these shared poems

- been shown where the art supplies are kept and where their Heart Books can be found.

Book Crates

Before the students start searching for poems, I make sure there are many poetry books available to them. I stack books in small crates on tables or counters that are easily accessible to the students. The categories in which you assemble books may be different from mine. Group books by topics you think are most compelling to your kids. Mine might be contemporary poets, classic poets, sports poems, art and poetry, love poems, poetry and the universe, or novels in verse. Or mix the books up in the crates.

I give a brief introduction of each crate or stack. As you move from stack to stack (crate to crate), show one poem from each crate—ones you know your kids will find compelling. Have this collection of poems (one from each stack) copied and in front of students as you move from crate to crate. Have them follow along as you read each poem aloud, one poem from each.

It is important for teachers to choose the books they believe their kids will be most attracted to and challenged by, and teachers need to think about poetry in the same way. Throughout this book you can see the tremendous variety of poems and range of poets my students find enjoyable, thought-provoking, and sometimes perplexing. You will begin to see that same variety as students recommend poets and poetry to each other and to you.

There are so many terrific books written by, or about, these poets that it is impossible to list them all. But these are some of the poets whose voices I would want in my classroom and you might begin to collect.

CONTEMPORARY POETS: Kwame Alexander, Maya Angelou, Sandra Cisneros, Billy Collins, Ralph Fletcher, Nikki Giovanni, Amanda Gorman, Nikki Grimes, Joy Harjo, Georgia Heard, Juan Felipe Herrera, Sara Holbrook, Caroline Kaufman, Rupi Kaur, Jane Kenyon, Ted Kooser, George Ella Lyon, Pat Mora, Walter Dean Myers, Marilyn Nelson, Naomi Shihab Nye, Mary Oliver, Andrea Davis Pinkney, Jack Prelutsky, Tupac Shakur, Shel Silverstein, Charles Simic, Clint Smith, Gary Soto, Kim Stafford, Jacqueline Woodson

NINETEENTH- AND TWENTIETH-CENTURY POETS: William Blake, Lucille Clifton, E. E. Cummings, Emily Dickinson, Rita Dove, Tom Feelings, Robert Frost, Chief Dan George, Donald Hall, Langston Hughes, Pablo Neruda, Mary Oliver, Edgar Allan Poe, Carl Sandburg, Shel Silverstein, William Shakespeare, William Stafford, Edna St. Vincent Millay, Walt Whitman, Richard Wilbur, William Carlos Williams (even earlier: Bashō [Japan] and Rumi [Persia])

COLLECTIONS: Poetry for Young People (each book focused on a different poet), published by Sterling Publishing Company in New York, are some of the best collections of classic poets. Other collections by Paul Janeczko, Naomi Shihab Nye, or Georgia Heard are all valuable additions.

I have listed novels in verse, sports poems, and spoken word poets in separate recommended lists at the end of this book.

Give students time to move from table to table to the collection most appealing to them or to saunter through your poetry collections in addition to those crates/stacks. I ask students to find their first poem from these collections. I want them to see the possibilities in the books we have. Once they have a poem that is somehow connected to something that matters most to them from their Heart Maps, they construct a double-page spread based on the instructions I have given them. (See the Appendix.)

Reading to Find a Poem

Students need to plan out the page after finding the poem. If they do not have time to write the poem into their Heart Book, have them write down the title of the poem they found, the title of the book in which they found it, and page number so they can find the poem again. If students have computers or phones, they may look up poems online, from suggested sites, such as The Writer's Almanac, American Life in Poetry, Poem-a-Day/poets.org, or poetry.org. In the Appendix, I have listed numerous resources available online that are valuable sources for finding poems and poets.

Students reading to find a poem

Students must handwrite or retype the poem they find. In doing this, they are paying closer attention to the title, the wording, the spacing, and the line breaks. They begin to notice things about the poem and ask themselves questions: *How did he come up with that title? In what ways is it connected to the poem? Why did she end the line with that word? Why no punctuation? What makes a stanza? Why some capitalization and others no capitalization?*

Although I am specific in my instructions to the students about what goes on each side of the double-page spread, in reality I am much more flexible. They can design the spread in any way they choose, so long as all the elements listed are within the two pages. I suggest students plan a rough layout in pencil of all the elements that need to be on the two pages—so they are easily readable and artistically organized. Any wording should be typed or in dark ink in the final layout.

Planning/Constructing Double-Page Spreads

We work on these Heart Books every six or seven weeks for a day or two or during any transition times that arise. Like everything else that happens at middle school, I am flexible. Time varies depending on what else is going on in class. After the students complete their first double-page spread and I have introduced them to a number of poets, we get into a routine. Each time we pick up the Heart Books as a whole class to do a second or third double-page spread, I introduce students to a new poet or poets by sharing one or two of their poems and giving the students a quick art lesson. (See Art Invitations in the Appendix.) If the poet is Mary Oliver or Pablo Neruda, I might show them a watercolor technique. Both poets frequently write about nature, and watercolor is a perfect medium to illustrate their poetry. Other times, the poets and art techniques may have nothing in common. It doesn't matter because once kids start working independently, the poets and the art techniques are all different.

Over the course of the year, the art techniques include contour drawing and watercolor, torn or cut paper, collage, Zentangles, and photography. Nothing complicated, as I am not an art teacher. But the students amaze me with their own art as much as they amaze me with their writing.

Students planning, laying out, and constructing double-page spreads

Core of the Heart Books

I think we actually need poetry. We need the immersive experience in our humanity that poetic language can give us . . . that allow(s) us to contemplate what matters in our lives. One new phenomenon that I've observed that goes to why we need poetry, is how much we love podcasts. How suddenly, in a world where we can be looking at a million screens at a time and multitasking our brains out, what we want is a human voice in our ear that actually pushes everything else away. (Podcasts) . . . provide a chamber for a certain kind of mental relaxation and exercise. And that is what poetry can do if one doesn't begin with a kind of coughing and sneezing, allergic, terrified reaction to it, or if one doesn't go lunging after the meaning. "What does this poem mean? I don't know!" or "I'm stupid. It's stupid. Goodbye." . . .

The experience of drawing students in to that refreshing kind of exercise of reading a poem, is the most important work I do. . . .

—Sarah Aronson, November 8, 2018, Montana Public Radio, Elisa New, PBS Host and Creator of "Poetry in America"

As students pour through poetry collections in my classroom, I ask them to read the poem aloud before they select it to include it in their Heart Book. How did it sound? What did they notice about pace and rhythm? What kind of feeling did they get from the way it sounded, the words used? As they read it aloud, could they show that feeling coming through in their voice? Each time I introduce them to a new poet, I try hard to capture the feeling with my voice and pacing.

When we read a poem aloud, we seldom talk about what the poet might have meant. We do not analyze the poem. We talk more about what it makes us think, what it makes us feel, and what we notice the poet does to make us think or feel that way. In the pages that follow showing the students' Heart Books, you will notice they are *responding* to the poems they chose. Responding, not analyzing. "The experience of drawing students in to that refreshing kind of exercise of reading a poem" (Aronson 2018) may be some of the most important work that we do.

Students' Reconstructed Heart Book Pages

Throughout this book I give examples of what a double-page spread looks like. All quite different. The students have to figure out an organizational pattern and layout that make the pages easy to read. On the instruction sheet in the Appendix, you can see what I expect the students to include on these two pages. To make these double-page spreads easier for you to read, I reconstructed them here, pulling from a considerable number of students' Heart Books what they did well to share as examples with your students. The pages you see here, in this section, are not the way they appeared in each student's Heart Book. *They are reformatted for your ease of reading.*

Trying to include an entire Heart Book was not possible, but hopefully what I chose to include will be helpful to you and your students. Each poem they are writing about was always in the Heart Book, but it is often not here in the shared pages (it is prohibitively expensive to gain permission to obtain the rights to publish some poems). What is most important is the student's response to the poem. In some cases, that response only makes sense with the poem, which I did try to include.

At the top of each student's page or pages, I listed what might be most helpful to notice. Regardless, everything on these pages is worthy of our attention. I was most impressed with the way so many students were motivated to go back to poems again and again, thinking through what they noticed the poet did that touched them personally or helped them garner ideas or craft moves for their own writing. It could be any of the following:

- the student's thoughts on the concept of "poetry" before and/or after doing the Heart Books
- what struck them about a particular poet
- their reaction and/or response to a particular poem
- personal connections brought to mind from the poem
- illustration/art techniques
- using the Heart Map for more fully developed pieces of writing.

In some cases, I added comments about what the student did especially well or what the student missed or could have done better. In this second case, it is clear to me, I am the one who missed the boat, by not taking the time to note more carefully what the student needed from me to help clarify their thinking and understandings. These comments on the student pages are in red, so you can distinguish my discoveries from their words. Each student's page is different, just as it was in their Heart Books.

Teacher Tip

As I reconstructed these pages, it occurred to me that it might be effective to have students go back into their Heart Books to find those things they did well and post them on what they might call a "Year-End Reflective Evaluation" of their discoveries about poetry and themselves. My students' reconstructed pages could be used as examples to show your students.

Thomas B.

RESPONSE TO POET: Charles Simic

ILLUSTRATIONS: pencil and pen sketches

THOUGHTS ON POETRY

WHAT I NOTICED ABOUT THOMAS' RESPONSE

"Listen" by Charles Simic

From That Little Something *(Simic 2008)*

RESPONSE: "Listen" explores the idea of unknown, or just ignored, consequences of your actions. That idea intrigued me, and lured me into a further analysis of the poem. The thought of ignored consequences is a thought that drifts into my head at night. In my past, I've said or done many things that I had not fully thought through, leading to consequences that I had not intended or expected to happen. Thinking about those mistakes leads me to regretting them.

Working in a bomb factory is an extreme example of how this can be applied to someone's life. The people know what they're making, bombs. But they don't imagine how they're used after production and how they will affect people. They try to ignore the obvious with the intention to make themselves feel better.

The couple working the night shift observes the child engulfed in flames, leaping from the window, surely to his or her death. Their consequences that were once ignored, are now being presented in a truly horrific fashion.

This poem forces me to rethink my decisions more thoughtfully than I have in the past. It urges me to wonder how my current and future actions will affect me in my life.

Illustrated response to "Listen" by Charles Simic

"Death's Book of Jokes" by Charles Simic

From That Little Something *(Simic 2008)*

RESPONSE: "Death's Book of Jokes" is about death, something that interests and scares me. At first glance, the first two stanzas reference and address the grim topic. They also contain numerous symbols of death, such as constant reminders of time, a touch on a church, and a mention of the Grim Reaper. But the last stanza takes an unexpected twist on this dark topic.

As Death approaches the protagonist, he is going to tell him it's "his time." The watch is then presented, surely showing him it's "his time," but rather than the protagonist reacting to Death, he ignores it and simply laughs at the price of the watch. In essence, he is standing up to Death, telling him it's not his time yet. Essentially a big "screw you" to Death.

Illustrated response to "Death's Book of Jokes" by Charles Simic

Death scares me, worries me, gives me anxiety. Who's not afraid of it? This poem shows me that I should not be afraid of death, but rather have Death reorganize his schedule around me.

In Simic's words: "Poetry is an orphan of silence. The words never quite equal the experience behind them."

"One writes because one has been touched by the yearning for, and the despair of, ever touching the Other."

After reading so many poems I realize that poetry makes me think of writers who pour out their heart and emotions. More heart and emotion than I initially thought.

Poetry finds a way to convey its theme in a more complex way than other genres of writing. Other writing will feed the events to the reader, while poetry will often convey it symbolically or through a metaphor, forcing the reader to think and analyze the piece more thoroughly. Poetry often requires multiple reads and careful analysis of the words the poet uses to fully understand the idea, or theme, behind the poem.

While crafting the Heart Book I stumbled on multiple poems by Charles Simic that impressed and interested me. . . . They all forced me to rethink how I will act in the future and they made me regret some of my past decisions.

Thomas B.

As I mentioned earlier in the book, it is a good idea to introduce your students to classic and contemporary poets from your state (from New Hampshire: Robert Frost, Donald Hall, Jane Kenyon, May Sarton, Charles Simic, Ralph Fletcher, just to name a few). Without the introduction, I am not sure that Thomas would have found Simic on his own. But his poetry struck a chord in this eighth grader. Simic's poems gave him pause to think about big ideas: ignored or unintended consequences of our actions, on a personal or world stage, and death.

I am impressed with how thoughtful and articulate Thomas is in his response to both poems. He chooses his wording carefully, the way poets do in their writing, showing us these poems "urge" him to think.

Briana B.

RESPONSE TO POETS: Jack Prelutsky and Amity Gaige

ART INVITATION: stick figures and cut paper

WHAT I NOTICED ABOUT BRIANA'S ILLUSTRATIONS

BEFORE DOING THE HEART BOOK I didn't know anything about poetry. I never knew that I could relate a poem to myself. Or really like a poem. When the Heart Book idea was first given to me, and I was told what needed to be in it, I was thinking, *this is going to be so hard, finding a poem that I like and one that relates to me.* But as the year passed and my Heart Book filled, I realized how much poetry could mean to me. I wrote about things I would never have thought about being related to a poem. For example, in my first poem "Rose Begonias," I related it to my Nana and great-grandmother. Also, in my fourth poem "Simple Request," I wrote about the three peach trees in our backyard.

I guess the reason I never knew much about poetry is because, in my life I never read much poetry. I never wanted to. Now, since I have thoroughly read many, many poems I feel that I now know poetry. I know how to relate to it and I know what I like.

Briana B. Heart Map

"I Am Tired of Being Little" by Jack Prelutsky

From Something Big Has Been Here *(Prelutsky 1990)*

I am tired of being little,
I am tired of being thin,
I wish I were giant size,
with whiskers on my chin.

No one would dare to tease me,
or take away my toys,
for I would be much bigger
than the bigger biggest "girls."

My folks would pay attention,
to every word I said,
they couldn't make me eat my peas,
or tell me "Go to bed!"

I'd never be afraid again,
if I were ten-foot-three,
I wish I were giant size,
instead of small like me.

When Jack Prelutsky was a child, he hated poetry. He couldn't stand it. He never thought he would ever become a writer or a poet. He discovered poetry when he was drawing imaginary creatures at age 24. He wrote things alongside the creatures. A friend suggested he show the pictures and writing to an editor. He did, and they liked them.

He gets his idea from EVERYTHING he hears, sees, even says. . . . His advice to writers: READ READ READ and WRITE WRITE WRITE!

RESPONSE: This poem made me think how short I really am. My head is up to a lot of people's noses or mouths. People say they wish they were short. But they don't . . .

Being shorter than your friends means you don't fit into their clothes, you don't look as old and mature as they do, and you're just short.

You can't reach things on the top shelf and you can't jump as high. You can't ride the same roller coasters as your friends because you're not as tall as the sign says you must be to ride this roller coaster.

In the poem the writer says he wants to be ten-foot-three. That would be just as weird. At this age, I would want to be five-foot-four.

My favorite line is, "My folks would pay attention to every word I said, they couldn't make me eat my peas or tell me "Go to bed!"

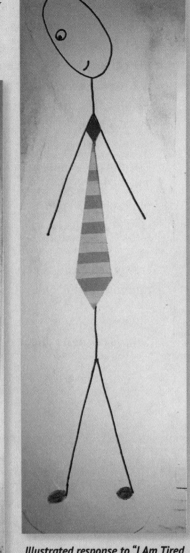

It is impressive that Briana found a way to illustrate each poem she chose in the simplest of ways, yet that way enhanced the idea of the poem. Stick figures and a blue watercolor wash on the page worked well. She used hyperbole—or exaggeration—in her drawings to emphasize what it's like to be sooooo short, or sooooo tall. She kept insisting she could not draw, yet what she did was so effective.

She placed the two figures looking at each other from the fold in each page with the writing in column format as per this page.

Illustrated response to "I Am Tired of Being Little" by Jack Prelutsky

Again, fearing her inability to draw, Briana realized she could make just as effective an illustration from cut paper in a way that enhanced the idea she took from the poem. Simple requests: the sunsets that "turn the sky nectarine colors" like orange and gold. The "crystal rain" and just one giant "peach without a worm." A bit of exaggeration in the size of the peach and worm emphasizes the simplicity of the poem and the simplicity of what one might ask God for.

The house we moved into came with three tiny peach trees in our back yard. Through years of nurturing and trimming the trees they now grow buckets of peaches.

After school my brother and sister and I race out to find the ripest fruit. When you find one without a worm you dig your teeth into it and the sweet juice crawls down your sleeve. You eat another and another and another, until your tummies are full and you sink into the hay bales and watch the sun go down.

Simple requests. Illustrations that enhance the simplicity of the words.

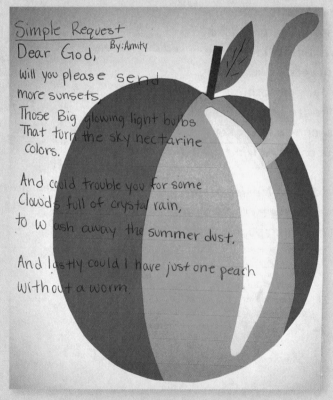

Briana's illustrated response to "Simple Request" by Amity Gaige"

Ailla C.

RESPONSE TO POETS: Silverstein, Poe, Fletcher, Frost, Sandburg
DESCRIPTION OF HEART MAP AND THOUGHTS ON POETRY
LAYOUT OF DOUBLE-PAGE SPREADS

Of importance to me on my heart map:

Music: playing the violin for more than ten years and the viola in the Boston Youth Symphony

Places: family cabin in Maine, Boston, church, school and home

Writing, reading, & art: I love books and writing my own stories.

Art (both traditional & digital): Art is my absolute favorite thing to do. I plan to study animation and eventually work as an animator. I love creating characters.

Rainbow Flag: I am close to people who are part of the LGBT community. I like them and am a supporter of equal rights for that group.

Nature & the Environment: *c*ritical issues important to my family

Sport: fencing

Technology: *I*t is both convenient and challenging.

Poetry means an idea, feeling, or image boiled down to its most basic form, where every word is crucial to rhythm, description, or something else. It is different from other kinds of writing because the focus isn't on wordy-ness or mechanics, necessarily, but on bringing across the purest essence of the poem's main idea.

Ailla C. Heart Map

"Every Thing on It" by Shel Silverstein

From Every Thing on It *(Silverstein 2011)*

RESPONSE: I've been reading Shel Silverstein's poems for a long time, and this is one of my very favorites. I love the way random objects can be pushed together with no real logic—and still make a good poem. The idea of so many unrelated things being part of one large object is intriguing to me. Also, I love how the poem calls out to be drawn. It's loads of fun to draw packed, detailed drawings. You can include so many little details, almost like inside jokes in a drawing.

"The Masque of the Red Death" by Edgar Allan Poe

From Poetry for Young People: Edgar Allan Poe *(Bagert 1995)*

RESPONSE: The thing that caught my eye (if that's the right term) is the way the words in this poem sound. They aren't all onomatopoeia, but they still have the tone of what they're describing. For example, "a dull, heavy, monotonous clang" is full of heavy words and monotonous sounds—long, drawn out, and laborious. "There came from the brazen lungs of the clock, a sound which was clear and loud and deep . . ."

Most of the important words in this sentence have short, hard syllables—crispy words, perfect to describe the penetrating sound of the clock.

Even the lines about the dancers, though they aren't describing a sound, still have a tone of uncertainty and lack of stability. I find the choice of words fascinating, in the way they convey more than just what they mean.

"daffodils" by Ralph Fletcher

From Ordinary Things *(Fletcher 1997)*

RESPONSE: Every one of this poem's four lines puts a picture in your head. First line tells you what they make—a little show. From there, each line mentions a color and the order is important. First yellow, the color you see first, putting on the show. Next, green—not bright like neon, but a saturated color. Last is brown, mellow, in the background, letting the yellow and green stand out, but certainly not lacking personality. It mentions things in this order: overview, foreground, middle ground, then background. I love how this poem is so short—it doesn't need any deep, philosophical meaning to be a well-crafted, beautiful poem.

"A Peck of Gold" by Robert Frost

From You Come Too *(Frost 1975)*

RESPONSE: I chose this poem because of the potential it has for symbolism and interpretation. It seems unlikely that kids would actually eat gold for obvious reasons, but there are many things it could be referring to: the dust cloud is like a person. Chaotic, could be, . . . Perhaps, "we all must eat our peck of gold" is saying that we should find—and make—a little good (gold) in every dust storm (person, object, event, situation, . . .). My life is certainly chaotic. There are so many things to do, so many places to be, like blowing dust. What is the gold? Maybe music, maybe art. Maybe helping other people. I'm not sure if I've "eaten" it yet.

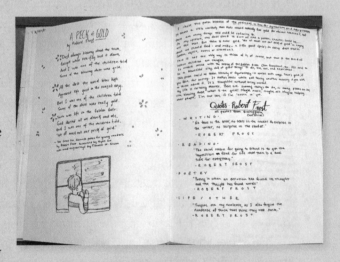

"From the Shore" by Carl Sandburg

From Poetry for Young People: Carl Sandburg *(Bolin 1995)*

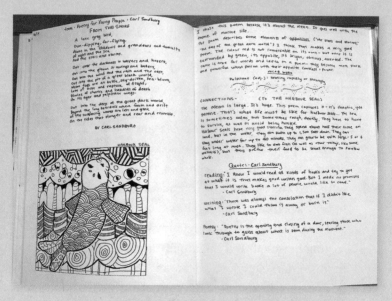

RESPONSE: The ocean is large. Huge. This poem captures it—it's chaotic, yet serene. That's what life must be like for harbor seals . . . the sea is sometimes calm, but sometimes rough, deadly. They have to hunt to survive, as well as avoid being hunted.

Harbor seals have very good stamina. They spend about half their time on land, but in the water, they can swim up to 1500 feet down. They can stay underwater for up to 40 minutes. They can grow to be quite large—five or six feet long, at most. They like to eat fish, and some mollusks, but they prefer their food to be small enough to swallow whole.

THOUGHTS ON POETRY: After reading a large quantity of poems from a variety of classic and contemporary poets, poetry makes me think of thought-provoking writing, but not necessarily written outright. You have to think carefully and examine it closely to find its meaning. It's not always long, and doesn't have to abide by all the rules of normal writing.

Poetry often has a flow and rhythm that isn't found in other kinds of writing. It's better read out loud, unlike many other forms of writing. It can also ignore regular rules of grammar, punctuation, and mechanics to some extent, which makes it all the more unusual.

One of my favorite poets is Edgar Allen Poe. I like how his poems are dark, bordering on mystical, and how they leave an impact after you read them. One can't easily forget the haunting "nevermore."

I also like Shel Silverstein. His poems are lighter in tone, but still quite strange. They're random. In another context, or by another writer, some of his topics would sound quite horrifying, but he manages to make them light-hearted and humorous.

Gwyneth C.

HEART MAP DESCRIPTION

RESPONSE TO POETS: **Becker, Silverstein, Dickinson, Doran**

CONNECTIONS: **poetry and the universe**

ART INVITATION: **Zentangle**

WHAT I MISSED IN GWYNETH'S READING AND RESPONSES

On my Heart Map:

Tree and mountains: The outdoors, especially forests like we have in NH, are a place of solace for me. Whether hiking, playing, fiddlehead picking, or just relaxing alone, I can unwind and feel in tune with the world, in a place where everything is at once familiar and new.

Bird: This bird is a variety called LBJs (Little Brown Jobs), which encompasses the vast majority of sparrow, finches and other small birds in winter. I aspire to continue my bird-watching hobby.

Musical Notes: As a singer, pianist, clarinetist, and one who is proficient at whistling when she should not be whistling, I am a musician.

Pencil: Creative writing is one of my favorite things to do. I also find school to be more of a blessing than a curse.

Computer: I have substantial interest in web design, programming, usability and Minecraft.

Right Triangle: I am a premature geometrician, member of last year's Mathcounts team and a firm believer in the saying that math is the language of science (my aspired profession).

Orchestra is possibly the best decision I've ever made.

Dragon: I am something of a v3.5 Dungeons & Dragons guru, and dragons are by far my favorite animal.

World in Thought Bubble: I think a lot about the "big picture," about things larger than me and my own life—the universe, different conceptions of God, and what in heck the future's going to be like.

Dancer: I just started dance this fall and it has been nothing short of therapeutic.

Book: Books were my first love, a passion which began in early elementary school and has never dwindled. Plunk me in a library and I could stay there all day.

Wizard's Staff: This is in homage to my penchant for RPG's (role-playing games), and also to my D & D character, Lia Dragontongue du Galarodel, who is a wizard and would use a staff like this.

When I hear the word *poetry*, I think of mostly beautiful words, lyrical and structureless, free to fly around your head in the most pleasant of ways. But also, more structured things, by virtue of symmetry or perfect meter, rather than language alone. The great poets are another thing: Shakespeare, Robert Frost, Edgar Allen Poe, . . .

Of all types of writing, poetry is perhaps the closest relation to music. Whether small and simple, as a haiku, or long as the Odyssey or Iliad, poems—at least the good ones—have cadence. It generally does not do for a poem to only look pretty, or have good meaning, it must sound pretty, to both listener and speaker.

I like Robert Frost, e.e. cummings, and Homer. Other than that though, I like whoever writes free verse and does it well. I like any poetry that deals with beauty in nature. And I suppose I should at least mention J.R.R. Tolkien's body of Elvish literature, which is a language that lends itself to poetry very well indeed!

"The Sadness Tree" by Abigail Lynne Becker

From A Box of Rain (Becker 1993)

RESPONSE: This poem literally made me cry. Mrs. Rief told the class about Abi, the author, who was killed on the last day of school, at the age of 16, in an automobile crash that was not her fault. I hate to do this—analyze the poem at all—because this is one of those times when prose is not enough, when the meaning runs deeper than words, and cannot be explained in a few sentences, though the sentences may be good ones that would be more than sufficient in another setting. . . . But I digress, though the digression is heartfelt.

This poem reminds me of the climbing maple in our backyard. It has been diseased for years, branches dying and leaves falling earlier each autumn. But the lowest few branches, the ones we liked best, have stayed. I was sad one day in fifth grade; the reason why has been lost to time. I was just crying, hugging the cool lichen-covered trunk, giving my sadness to the tree. I talked to it like a trusted friend. There was a feeling of words to the stillness, of silent communication. I could have sworn the tree listened.

The tree blew down a month or two ago, in a windstorm. It was dying anyway; how else would a tree go? I never hung a rope on it. "But it will never be the same."

In Abigail Becker's words: "I care about success, and worry about failure. I am constantly dealing with my fears through writing. My parents take my success in school extremely seriously. This causes me to worry not only about doing well, but it also makes me worry about pleasing them. Poetry is my gateway to success. I use writing as a way to feel good about myself."

"Invitation" by Shel Silverstein

From Where the Sidewalk Ends (Silverstein 1974)

RESPONSE: This poem is my every day. "Pretender," in some ways, fits me perfectly. I act, I role-play, I hide my love of Star Wars from nearly everybody. I sometimes forget that the real world exists. I wish there was actually someplace I could go, to simply stay for hours with the words, and the worlds behind them. Nobody else, just me and my fictions. You know how hard it is for me to resist the "flax-golden tales" sometimes. They beckon, "come in, come in," and the next thing I know I'm in trouble for reading or daydreaming during class.

Ah, the joys of an overactive imagination.

"Their Height in Heaven Comforts Not (696)" by Emily Dickinson

From Selected Poems of Emily Dickinson *(Dickinson 1994)*

RESPONSE: I often find with Emily Dickinson poems that some of them are easier to understand than others. This is one of the tougher sort. I found it in a book of Emily Dickinson, after a long and somewhat confusing search, and even had far too long (as in past the due date—oops!) to mull it over. I still can only get the gist of it. Emily seems to be talking about knowledge very transcendentally, as a superior alternative to material wealth. In some ways I agree with her. I take knowing things very seriously (as is probably obvious to you now!), and if stories like Ali Baba are any indication, money can be quite troublesome, especially when morals and a genie or two get involved.

I especially like the bits about "I'm finite. I can't see," and "This timid life of evidence/Keeps pleading, I don't know." It's my belief that while science is fascinating, it is in no way perfect; there are things out there it couldn't explain if it tried. Magic? God? Dark energy? The Force? Who knows? I certainly don't but nevertheless I believe there are mysteries yet to be solved that are perhaps unsolvable. Life would be boring without them.

"Horseshoe Crab" by Joel Doran

From https://Poemhunter.com

RESPONSE: You would not believe how hard it is to find a poem about a horseshoe crab, let alone a living one. Two other poems I found had everything to do with a dying, upside down horseshoe crab, but those definitely did not fit my tastes nor did they fit my zentangle (in which the crab is most certainly right side up!). This poem, I believe, talks about more than the crabs and the ocean: it talks about time and the fact that, yes, horseshoe crabs have been around for millions upon millions of years, giving evolution the cold shoulder. Personally, I find it fascinating that an organism can remain virtually unchanged for that long. How well-adapted must they be to ocean life for countless mutations to be beaten down by natural selection in favor of what already exists? Are horseshoe crabs an evolutionary pinnacle, a bottom-dwelling apotheosis of some sort?

This poem reads like something for a school assignment. I see at least two facts about horseshoe crabs worked in there, coupled with florid wording to mask them somewhat. In my experience, poetry and science don't mix—science is too uptight and cynical for poetry, and poetry is too indistinct and too often fictional for science. It's kind of a shame, as I have something of a passion for both. All in all, this is not the best poem, but it's special all the same. What else but poetry can conjure up images of stars and mountains and time itself, visions in burgundy and utmost calm, on the simple subject of a horseshoe crab?

If I had read Gwyneth's comments more carefully, or now I am wondering if I read them at all, I could have shared with her the incredible coupling of science and poetry. The Marginalian by Maria Popova is a site Gwyneth might enjoy for the science/poetry connections, where astrophysicist and author Janna Levin often discusses and reads poetry. Her reading of W. S. Merwin's "Berryman" is particularly moving, and can be found online. For the last several years scientists and poets have gathered for a celebration of The Universe in Verse: a celebration of science and nature through poetry (2019). At this event (annually at the end of April), poems such as "When I Heard the Learn'd Astronomer" by Walt Whitman, "Hubble Photographs: After Sappho" by Adrienne Rich, "My God, It's Full of Stars" by Tracy K. Smith, and "Figures of Thought" by Howard Nemerov, along with poems by Pablo Neruda, James Baldwin, Rachel Carson, and many others are read by astronomers, astrophysicists, poets, and musicians. I need to bring more of these readings into class for the students to see and hear the connections between poetry and the universe. Not just for Gwyneth, but for all of us.

James G.

Before doing the Heart Book I thought that poetry was a bit dull, and kind of pointless. My parents have poetry books, and I tried to read them once, but they didn't make sense. Confused me. Used weird words. I didn't get them. So then I stereotyped, and assumed all poetry was stupid because I did not understand it. I knew that there were famous poets like Emily Dickinson and Robert Frost, but I assumed that their poetry was stupid like the rest of them.

"Finale" by Pablo Neruda

From The Poetry of Pablo Neruda *(Neruda 2003)*

RESPONSE: I really could relate to the way he described losing a loved one. I don't know if that is what he meant in the poem, but when I first read it, I interpreted it as something someone would write to a lost one who was loved very much. I lost my grandmother, Nonna, three years ago, and I still think about her a lot. We were close, and I was hurt and upset when she died. I cried and cried, and blamed it on her, because I was young and didn't know better. I blamed her for leaving me, for not living forever like I hoped. But eventually I moved on and learned to see the good of being able to even spend that much time with her. When I read this poem, it was like reading a beautiful description of what I learned. Several of his lines almost made me cry because that's exactly what I was feeling after her death. I wish I could have told her that.

About Neruda: His father disapproved of his writing and literature, which is why he changed his name from Neftali Ricardo Reyes Basoalto to Pablo Neruda, so his father would not know it was his writing when it was published.

Neruda always wrote in green ink, as it was the color of hope.

"What the Janitor Heard on the Elevator" by Barbara Kingsolver

From Another America *(Kingsolver 1998)*

RESPONSE: I chose this poem because I think it talks about racism and all the issues that go with it. I especially like the way Kingsolver conveys the message though. She never says the word racism, or even hints outright that any racism is involved. But the mood of the poem is clear in the way that the two women talk about what the reader has to assume is a servant of some sort—he has to find another one who speaks English, and all in front of the janitor, without ever considering who he is or his feelings. All of these details in what they say adds up to one deep topic.

I agree with Kingsolver. Completely. Racism is a serious topic. All around the world racism is still a huge problem. In the poem people aren't being killed by the millions, or there is no mass genocide happening, but, just little comments, little conspiracies, little beliefs show the extreme prejudice. The little things add up, and they make for a hateful world.

In Kingsolver's words: "Close the door. Write with no one looking over your shoulder. Don't try to figure out what other people want to hear from you; figure out what you have to say. It's the one and only thing you have to offer."

"Balances" by Nikki Giovanni

From https://Poemhunter.com

RESPONSE: One of the reasons why I really like this poem is because of the way it is written. Nothing is capitalized. . . . She is blunt. Honest. Upfront. Most poets write with lots of metaphors and allusions, and the reader ends up being confused at the end. But not Giovanni. Not any of that fancy stuff. Only the cold, hard, brutal facts. Which really got the point across better than any reference ever could. The poem made me hurt for the author, and made me think about my relationships with other people. Do I still talk to this person? Do I lead them on, pretending to be a friend?

The way Giovanni writes is the way I want to write, try to write. To write with so much feeling that readers can relate and empathize with what I'm trying to say. If I could write poetry, this is the kind of poetry I would try to write.

In Giovanni's words: "There is always something to do. There are hungry people to feed, naked people to clothe, sick people to comfort and make well. And while I don't expect you to save the world, I do think it's not asking too much for you to love those with whom you sleep, share the happiness of those you call friend, engage those among you who are visionary and remove from your life those who offer you depression, despair and disrespect."

"Saturday at the Canal" by Gary Soto

From Who Will Know Us? *(Soto 1990)*

RESPONSE: I chose this poem because Soto talks about wanting freedom. He wants to get out of town, saying it while noticing the river "racing" away from town. To be honest, I feel like that too. All my life I've had to listen to what adults tell me to do, follow instructions from people with more "authority" than I have. Sometimes I feel like screaming and running, running until there is nowhere left to go. I want to live my life. Make choices for myself. I'm not saying I can live on the street by myself or run around wild in the woods, but I would appreciate some freedom once in a while. Not parents telling me to clean my room, time to eat, do this, do that. The more you push me to clean my room, the more I push back and resent it. Respect and a little freedom, that's all I ask.

Soto says it much more beautifully than I do. He makes you feel empathy for him. He take his problem and shouts it to the world silently, with pen and paper. Could that be me some day?

In Soto's words: "I'm a listener. I hear lines of poetry issue from the mouths of seemingly ordinary people. And, as a writer, my duty is not to make people perfect, particularly Mexican Americans. I'm not a cheerleader. I'm one who provides portraits of people in the rush of life."

"The Oldest Child" by Charles Simic

From **That Little Something** *(Simic 2008)*

RESPONSE: I like this poem—because I am the oldest child—even though I don't quite get it. I have an idea about what Simic is trying to say, but I don't fully understand it. I think he is trying to say that being the oldest child isn't easy. You may be the oldest but you still feel alone in the dark. I feel like no one gets me, no one in my family understands what I'm thinking or going through. Simic seems to understand and I feel empathy from him when I read this poem. Being the oldest doesn't mean that the night doesn't frighten you.

What I know not to do is automatically assume the poem is awful because I don't understand it.

In Simic's words: "Poetry: three mismatched shoes at the entrance of a dark alley."

"Lyric poets are always corrupting the young, making them choke in self-pity and indulge in reverie. Dirty sex and disrespect for authority is what they have been whispering into their ears for ages."

AFTER THE HEART BOOK: Since doing the Heart Book I learned that poetry has a deeper meaning. Well, good poetry, well-written poetry. I noticed that if you become open to new ideas and ways of expressing these ideas, then suddenly poetry becomes not only bearable, but likeable, and thoroughly enjoyable! I learned to love poetry, and although I don't always understand the poetry I read, I learned to accept it and interpret it in my own way. I also noticed that many poets have underlying themes, and that if you can grasp those themes, you can understand the poetry much better.

In his freshman year at a local private school, James, and several of his classmates, whom I had also had in eighth grade, invited me to a poetry reading by Jimmy Baca. James also knew I had worked with Baca at the Boothbay Literacy Retreat in Maine the preceding summer. As we were sitting in the auditorium, James sitting on my right, waiting for Baca to be introduced, my curiosity got the better of me and I said to James: "I've always wondered, in your Heart Book from last year, you read a wide variety of poets and wrote quite a bit of thoughtful response to each of them. But one of them you said little about. As a matter of fact, it was a Baca poem. I don't suppose you remember it."

"You mean 'Green Chili'?" he said. "Yes, I do remember it!"

I was surprised he remembered it. I shouldn't have been. The poem is provocative and rather suggestive of sexual innuendoes that made me a bit uncomfortable when I read the poem in James' Heart Book. I was glad he had not written much response to it, as I'm not sure how I would have responded. I should have let the conversation drop right there. But, I did not.

"So, . . . did you get a sense of what Baca might have been meaning to get at in this poem?" I asked.

"Oh, I'm pretty sure I understood what he was trying to get at!" he said. I decided not to ask what he understood. A few seconds passed as we waited in silence for Baca's reading. James turned to me and asked, "So, Mrs. Rief, . . . did you get it?"

Aaron H.

DESCRIPTION OF HEART MAP
ILLUSTRATION TECHNIQUES: **drawing**
WHAT I NOTICED/MISSED IN AARON'S RESPONSES

AN IMPORTANT ITEM ON MY HEART MAP is the cello. Music has always been part of my life, having first played the piano, then trumpet, then settling with cello. I love the deep and dreary sound the instrument can make. It is sad, but filled with meaning. On the cello I include the logos of two bands, Fall Out Boy and Panic! At the Disco. The two bands create music that can make you think for hours. There is also the first measure of cello music for the first Panic! At the Disco song I ever listened to.

I added a paintbrush and paint to represent drawing with my dad and sisters when we were younger. My sisters and I were dedicated when it came to art, using our whole basement as a studio. We would also be very excited whenever dad drew with us on the kitchen counter. I drew the classic video camera to represent movies. Watching movies with my family happens often and is when we can all relax together. On Demand is our savior.

There is also each species of pet I own: two donkeys, four sheep, one dog, three rabbits, and three ferrets. They are all important to me and inspired my passion for zoology. There is also a beluga whale, since the melon-headed sea creature is my favorite animal. It brings back my best memory of swimming with belugas, and listening to the kids' song "Baby Beluga" when I was little with my mom.

Lastly, I included a tree with clouds and the sun. I have always loved nature and the forest, having done an ecological camp called Coyote Club since first grade. I also covered the background with blues to represent water and the ocean, since I have always felt a connection to water as an element.

When I hear the word "poetry," I think of many emotions scribed on a page. It focuses on an event and everything you felt during the event. Poetry is different because there is no "correct" format for a lot, but there are strict formats for others, even down to the number of syllables. Poetry seems to flow when read aloud. One poet I remember reading a lot, is Shel Silverstein. He wrote many distinctive poems about the craziest things and I still remember them.

"A Dream Within a Dream" by Edgar Allan Poe

From Poetry for Young People: Edgar Allan Poe (Bagert 1995)

RESPONSE: I constantly worry about the world around me. Where are we? Why are we here? Are there more universes? This poem "A Dream Within a Dream" indirectly asks questions like these. Are we dreaming right now? Have we never woken up? This poem leaves you with many questions, although Poe answers none. . . .

I noticed Poe repeats the same two lines at the end of each stanza. "In all we see or seem, Is but a dream within a dream," is now stuck in my head as I think about the poem. The title repeats the main idea. Are we ever in reality?

This poem also mentions "Grains of golden sand—How few! Yet how they creep through my fingers to the deep, while I weep—while I weep!" These grains of sand still fall through his hand no matter how hard he tries (to stop them). I later read that these golden grains of sand represent his life, and he can't control time. His life will end no matter how hard he tries (to stop it). No matter how hard we all try, we can't stop the flow of time.

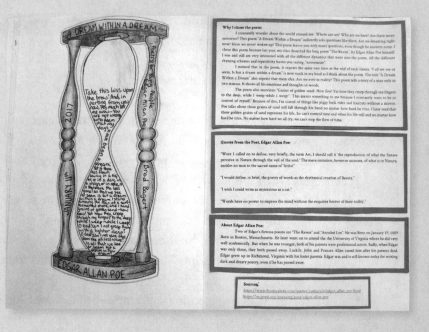

"Jabberwocky" by Lewis Carroll

From Poetry for Young People: Lewis Carroll
(Mendelson and Copeland 2008)

RESPONSE: *Alice in Wonderland* was one of the first Disney movies I remember watching. I vividly remember sitting on my parents' bed and staring at the small grey television. . . . I was quite scared of the Cheshire Cat and his toothy grin.

Made up words fill the writing. Just reading this poem of gobbledygook messes with your brain. . . . Even though many of the words are hard to understand, you still know what is happening in the poem.

Like many poems, the stanza at the beginning is the same one at the end, to try and stick it in your head. This poem wants to be remembered.

My favorite genre has always been fantasy. On my heart map I have symbols of different fandoms in a cloud. These fandoms represent my love for literature and complex fantasy worlds.

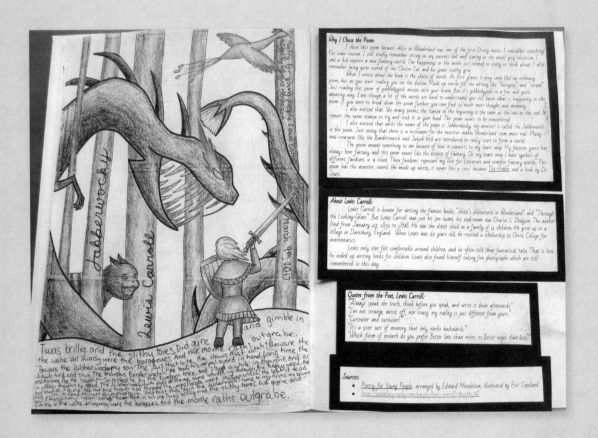

"Sheep" by Carl Sandburg

From Poetry for Young People: Carl Sandburg *(Bolin 1995)*

RESPONSE: My mind never seems to be able to settle down, so I have a hard time sleeping. I lay my head down, close my eyes, but I involuntarily can't stop thinking. No matter how much desire I have to sleep, I can't. When I was little I would try counting sheep, which did help me fall asleep.

I noticed that this poem often repeats itself. In the first stanza, almost every other phrase starts with "one by one," with dashes between each phrase. There is a lot of description of the sheep in that first stanza also—how they walk, how they jump, how their hooves sound . . .

This poem reminds me how much animals have always meant to me. Once we moved into our 100-year-old farmhouse we wanted animals: two donkeys, three rabbits, three ferrets, a dog, and four sheep: Phineas, Ferb, Jazzy, and Mamao.

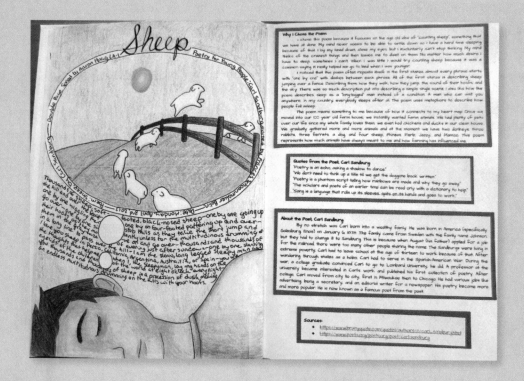

"The Tide Rises, The Tide Falls"
by Henry Wadsworth Longfellow

From Poetry for Young People: Henry Wadsworth Longfellow
(Schoonmaker 1998)

RESPONSE: The blob fish, the animal I am studying in marine biology, is a gelatinous animal that dwells on the ocean floor. The blob fish is commonly seen as extremely ugly because of the way it "melts" when taken out of the ocean's high pressure.

The poem repeats the line "the tide rises, and the tide falls" four times. The poem tells the story of the cycle of the tide. Day turns to night, and then morning. The night falls, the footprints in the sand are erased by the waves, and day takes over the sky again.

I have always loved the ocean. When I was younger I would pretend to be a water-bender (a human with hydrokinetic powers). . . . Ever since then I have loved everything about water, marine animals, lakes, oceans, swimming. The career paths I am strongly considering are marine biology, or oceanography. I want to study everything about the ocean, a force that takes up 71% of the earth's surface.

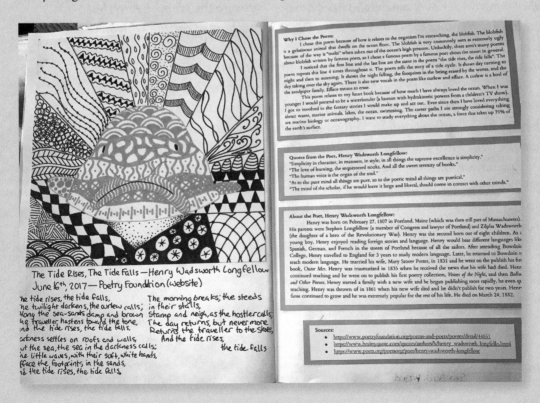

Now that I've read so many poems, when I hear the word *poetry* I think of writing that perfectly captures emotions. Everything about poetry is there for a reason.

My favorite poet is Edgar Allen Poe. I really like his dark and gloomy themes and how none of his poems are supposed to be happy.

What I noticed about Aaron's work: He is a talented artist, with a natural ability for drawing. I think I was so impressed with Aaron's art that I paid more attention to his illustrations than his thinking about the poems. He is meticulous in his organization and layout and attempts to make personal connections to each poem he chose. He chose classical poets, looking for challenges they might present. He was intentional in the way he incorporated the poem into his illustration to really weave the words and pictures together. As well as reading a variety of poets, he chose a variety of techniques to illustrate his understanding of each poem.

He recognizes some of the craft moves in the poems—such as repetition, unique wording, line breaks, and layout on the page. He could have attempted to explain what those craft moves did to him as a reader or in what ways they may have emphasized an idea in the poem. I realize now that I needed to be more explicit in showing the students how to do that with an example from a poem I was sharing with them. What craft moves does the poet make? What do those craft moves do to the writing and/or to the reader?

Note to self/note to teachers: Show students how to recognize craft moves in several poems, name those moves or techniques, and name what they do to the writing and/or to the reader. In Aaron's case, we could have talked about what the repetition seemed to do, or the specific unique words the poet chose, or the effect of the line breaks. Because Aaron does not see the intentionality behind some of the decisions in the writing, he interprets it as "no guidelines, no structure, and no requirements for spelling, grammar or punctuation in poetry."

Carly H.

"Shyness" by Pablo Neruda

From The Dreamer *(Ryan 2010)*

I scarcely knew, by myself, that I existed,
that I'd be able to be, and go on being.
I was afraid of that, of life itself.
I didn't want to be seen,
I didn't want my existence to be known.
I became pallid, thin, and absentminded.
I didn't want to speak so that nobody
would recognize my voice, I didn't want
to see so that nobody would see me.
Walking, I pressed myself against the wall
like a shadow slipping away. . . .

RESPONSE: I chose this poem because it stood out to me when it was read in class. I loved the way he described what he was feeling and how his words flowed and fit together like puzzle pieces.

I could relate to this pain because I myself am pretty shy as well. I felt like I could connect with every line he wrote.

I also find Neruda's story really interesting. How his father wanted him to be anything but what he was—a writer. How his father burned all of his writing and made him stay in bed for days. All of it very unfortunate, tragic even, but Neruda makes it beautiful in the way that he writes. His poetry has such unbelievable purpose and character and voice. I feel like I know him, as if he is speaking right to me when I read his work. I can confidently say he is my favorite poet.

Even his short little blurbs about life are beautiful with meaning and power. I plan to find more of his work and continue to learn more about him.

In Pablo Neruda's words: "I grew up in this town. My poetry was born between the hill and the river. It took its voice from the rain, and like the timber, it steeped itself in the forests."

"The books that help you most are those which make you think the most. The hardest way of learning is that of easy reading; but a great book that comes from a great thinker is a ship of thought, deep freighted with truth and beauty."

"A child who does not play is not a child, but the man who doesn't play has lost forever the child who lived in him and who he will miss terribly."

Carly H. Heart Map

Mia H.

LAYOUT OF DOUBLE-PAGE SPREADS

ART INVITATIONS: watercolor, sketching, and Zentangle

WHAT I NOTICED/MISSED IN MIA'S RESPONSE TO POEMS

Mia H. Heart Map

"Flying at Night" by Ted Kooser

From Good Poems, American Places *(Keillor, 2011)*

RESPONSE: I love flying at night, seeing the stars and all the cities lit up underneath us. I noticed the poem uses metaphors, "a galaxy disapppears the way a snowflake does when it hits water. " Very softly, and nobody notices. I noticed all the details about stars and space, like the shimmering novas, constellations and galaxies.

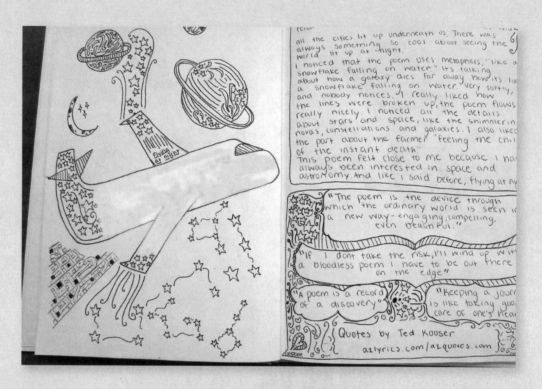

What Mia misses—the farmer snaps on his lights after feeling the chill of that distant death of a galaxy and drawing his small world together in the light of his care. Do we even notice, the grandeur of it all? She begins to notice but then lets it go. . . . My fault . . . never made the time to talk with her.

"Why I Am Happy" by William Stafford

From Learning to Live in the World *(Stafford 1994)*

RESPONSE: I can relate to the feeling of happiness the poet is feeling. I love poems about happiness and good feelings. Sometimes it's nice to just stop and try to feel happy. . . . I love nature and admiring nature's beauty, which is something this poem conveys.

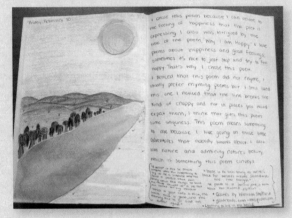

Mia only talks about liking happy poems. She never notices what makes Stafford happy—the lake is "so blue, and nobody owns it . . . a willow listens gracefully. . . . That lake stays blue and free" despite the turning of the world (and all that means) and Stafford knows where that lake is. If she had related to the title of the book, Learning to Live in the World, *she might have made more connections to what we are doing to the earth. My fault for not helping her see this.*

"Sounds Like Pearls" by Maya Angelou

From Just Give Me a Cool Drink of Water 'fore I Die *(Angelou 2003)*

RESPONSE: The English language is amazing/interesting and this poem intrigued me because it is about sounds. I don't understand the metaphor "sounds like pearls" because it doesn't seem like pearls would be used to explain sound, but maybe they are used because they roll. There are some rhyming words like ear, fear, disappear.

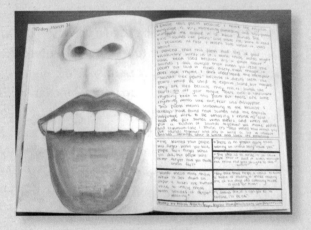

Mia struggles with this poem but never asks big questions of herself. If we had talked through the previous two poems she collected, she might have seen more in this poem. Time—there is not enough of it.

"Pink Flamingo" by A. P. Taylor

From https://hellopoetry.com (2015)

RESPONSE: I like how the lines of this poem are short and quick. There aren't a lot of metaphors or similes. It has some good describing adjectives, which help me visualize the poem.

I like flamingoes. I love how they all bond together and I love their pink color, which comes from their diet. They were one of the first species of bird, more than 30-50 million years old.

Mia missed that this is a fake flamingo and what the poet might be saying about them. If I had made the time to talk through big ideas in previous poems, she might have seen more on her own.

I learned from Mia's Heart Book that she is a talented artist, who is creative and imaginative. She tried a variety of different techniques for each illustration: sketching, contour drawing, watercolor, pencil drawing, Zentangle, . . . all of them quite successfully. She is neat and careful in both organization and layout. She read a good variety of contemporary poets.

When she connects to the poems it seems to be because of what she considers the topic, without delving into something deeper, a big idea behind the topic. She did not use any of the lines or formats of the poems to draw understanding or big ideas beyond the literal. I wish she had given each poem a bit more thought into the feeling she could have drawn from each if she had questioned herself with: **What is the poet trying to say about _____?** *If I had read her response to the first poem more carefully, I think I could have nudged her into a closer reading and deeper thinking.*

Kathy M.

RESPONSE TO POET: **Kwame Alexander**

ART INVITATION: **watercolor**

RESPONSE: I never expected the authors of sports books to have any writing that would interest me. But, out of ideas, I picked up a book of poems by Kwame Alexander and was blown away. His writing about love and other very raw emotions was the type of writing that leaves you speechless, rethinking your existence. This poem speaks to me because love *is* a sort of second gravity, almost stronger than the kind that keeps us on the ground.

In the poet's words:

"That's all you hope for from a book—that it's going to resonate with young people and empower them in some way. I believe poetry can get kids reading."

Elise R.

RESPONSE TO POETS: Naomi Shihab Nye, Carl Sandburg
ART INVITATION: watercolor, pastels

Elise R., Heart Map

"Visiting My Old Kindergarten Teacher, Last Day of School" by Naomi Shihab Nye

From A Maze Me (Nye 2005)

RESPONSE: I chose this poem for two reasons. First, it reminds me of the last day of school saying goodbye to all of my teachers. The sadness, joy, and scared all circling the room. Sad that you are saying goodbye to your favorite teachers. Joy that it is finally summer and there is no more homework. Scared about the new school year that looms just over summer. Will the teachers be nice?

I also chose the poem for another meaning hidden behind the words. The teacher watches as her students continue to leave her and she has to start fresh again for another year. It reminds me of moving. I left all my friends and anything familiar and had to start brand new. The poem shows the passing of time and that there is nothing we can do to stop it.

I noticed that the poem is written so that it doesn't give the teacher a face, but leaves it up to you to picture one of your own teachers that you said goodbye to. For me, at least, this made me think of Mr. Pope, who was my art teacher 4th, 5th, and 6th grades. He was the hardest to say goodbye to.

Also, the poem mentions a few items that she puts away. For me, that reminds me of things I don't do anymore, packed away in the back of my brain. . . . The beginning of the poem is focused on both student and teacher. By the end of the poem it focused only on the teacher. (The students are gone.)

In the words of Naomi Shihab Nye:

> **"If a teacher told me to revise, I thought that meant my writing was a broken-down car that needed to go to the repair shop. I felt insulted. I didn't realize the teacher was saying, 'Make it shine. It's worth it.' Now I see revision as a beautiful word of hope. It's a new vision of something. It means you don't have to be perfect the first time. What a relief!"**
>
> **"I love the solitude of reading. I love the deep dive into someone else's story, the delicious ache of a last page."**

"Buffalo Dusk" by Carl Sandburg

From Poetry for Young People: Carl Sandburg *(Bolin 1995)*

RESPONSE: I chose this poem because of animal extinction. Buffaloes were one of the first animals to be on the verge of extinction from over-hunting and human mistakes. There used to be many buffalo but now there are so few. (They are coming back, due to protection in the national parks.) There are so many other species gone, due to human mistakes. Soon these animals will be forgotten in all but bones and artwork. The people who saw them will be gone. We need to learn from our mistakes.

I noticed that the first two lines also end the poem. Sandburg probably did this to remind us again that the buffalo were nearly gone, so near extinction, and that we must remember them through more than artwork, by keeping them alive. The poet reminds us that they are magnificent beasts to make us want to see them in real life.

The poem made me think of other animals today that are on the verge of extinction and are magnificent just like the buffalo. It made me want to protect them so future generations wouldn't have to rely on just artwork.

Buffalo Dusk
By Carl Sandburg
From Book of Animal Poetry

The buffaloes are gone.
And those who saw the buffaloes are gone.
Those who saw the buffaloes by the thousands and how they
    pawed the prairie sod into dust with their hoofs,
    their great heads down pawing on in a great pageant
    of dusk.
Those who saw the buffaloes are gone.
And the buffaloes are gone.

In the words of Naomi Shihab Nye:

> **"As a direct line to human feeling, empathetic experience, genuine language and detail, poetry is everything that headline news is not. It takes us inside situations, helps us imagine life from more than one perspective, honors imagery and metaphor—those great tools of thought—and deepens our confidence in a meaningful world."**

Hunter R.

I don't have a lot of favorite poets. For that matter, I don't really have any poets.

After doing the Heart Book I realize poetry tends to be different from other writing because, more often than not, a poem is a metaphor for something a lot more important.

I'm still not huge on poetry and I still don't have a favorite poem or poet, although I will say that I have started to grow on poetry.

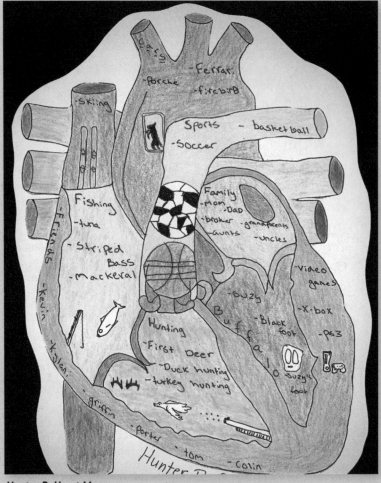

Hunter R. Heart Map

"Sunset" by Ralph Fletcher

From Have You Been to the Beach Lately? *(Fletcher 2001)*

The sun dips
    to its lowest point,
painting the sky in colors you can't
find in any box of crayons.

Magenta goes to extraterrestrial pink
and rays like spun silver introduce
a new kind of light
to the world.

The sun touches the horizon
lighting a brilliant path
from us to our star,
a fiery core of gold.

We stand without speaking,
Dad puts his arms around Mom,
Ben says: *I see my soul, dancing.*

RESPONSE: When we go tuna fishing we always leave early. At about 6:15 a.m. the most unbelievable view is waiting there for us. It's like the sun and sky are rising from the Atlantic. I wish it would stay like that all the time. The image reminds me of Robert Frost's poem in *The Outsiders* (Hinton, 1967)—"Nothing Gold Can Stay." These are the colors we often see as we head out tuna fishing. But they only last a few seconds. I enjoy this poem by Ralph Fletcher, not because it is sunset but I prefer to think of it as sunrise. The description in the poem, especially "magenta goes to extraterrestrial pink," is striking to me. Ralph Fletcher said, "The real meaning of a poem is to stop time." This poem does that even though the real sunrise or sunset disappears so quickly.

"Outside" by William Stafford

From The Way It Is *(Stafford 1998)*

RESPONSE: Coyotes are a threat to what we love, the buffalo. They are a pain to deal with. A nuisance to our property and the buffalo. Coyotes are very intelligent and can outwit whatever they want. Almost every night in bed I get up and open the window and listen to the coyotes howl for nearly a half hour. They yelp. They howl. They bark. I wonder what they are saying to each other? I wonder what they found or why they are howling?

"Fight of a Buffalo with Wolves" by James McIntyre

From https://poeticous.com

RESPONSE: This poem means a lot to me and my family because we own buffalo and they are one of my favorite animals. They are huge with a lot of mass and are hard to take down. But in this poem the huge bull is confronted by one, then two, and then an entire pack of wolves. He kills several "with horn and hoof" but there are too many of them and they have torn his hide.

This past year we had a baby buffalo that could not milk and almost died. Her name is Suzy. My favorite buffalo. . . . This poem relates to Suzy because you understand how close to death you actually are. Every one of us is vulnerable. Though buffalo are big, majestic beasts, they have their weaknesses like the rest of us.

"For Bow Hunters Only" by Hunter R.

I stopped; everything slowed down in a fast way. Time warped. Seconds felt like hours, and minutes, days. Slowed down. Stopped. I reached for the bow in one slow movement. As time moved on, so did the deer that was soon to find its faith. He inched his way with a broad, stalky walk that showed his confidence and caution. Every muscle in his neck moved to hear the slightest sound. Antlers tall, body thick with muscle and mass. Carelessly hitting branches, he crashed through, as if looking for a fight. Standing broadside, looking left, he listened. He took a step, and I drew. His vitals filled the sights as the pin lay behind his shoulder. With the snap of the bow, time froze as I watched my arrow spin toward the target and sink in, slicing the flesh like butter, thrusting all the way through. Blood poured out of him like a pitcher full of water. He dropped, taking his last breath.

RESPONSE: This poem, which I wrote because I couldn't find one about bow hunting, means a lot to me because I took up bow hunting this past year and really enjoy it. It takes a lot more skill than gun hunting, and you earn a lot more respect as a hunter. I enjoy writing quick descriptive pieces like this because, other than family, only two things matter: hunting and fishing. It's a time to get away because nature and animals have no drama. It's a place for me to clear my head.

"Out Fishing" by Barbara Howes

From American Sports Poems *(Knudson and Swenson 1995)*

RESPONSE: In Howes' poem, the "big one" engages in a tug-of-war with the fisherman, and of course, dives and snaps the line. So true, so often, for us too.

Today's Catch by Hunter R.: At 3:00 AM the day starts. Roll out of bed. Eat a quick breakfast, get in the car, and head to the dock. As the engines start I crawl onto the boat, exhausted. Rolling waves that crash against the boat make moving hard. I try to make my way to the front of the boat to find more acceptable seating.

As the waves grow bigger, the white caps launch higher into the sky, a mini-volcano that suppresses itself under the wave. When you look out all you see is ocean, as far as the eye can see. Welcome to fishing.

The stench of dead fish rolls by as we pass a fishing vessel. Fish lurk underneath their boat in blood-drenched water from the ship. Whales lunge for the sky as they crash with a tremendous wave. When we reach the Isle of Shoals, we drop lines for mackerel. The mackerel catch our hooks as if we are using a net; they pile up in overflowing buckets that pour over the edges, flopping for their lives as their gills search for water.

When we have caught enough mackerel to last us through the day, we head out to our spot. While others set the tuna lines, I drop my own line trying to avoid the gut-wrenching feeling of seasickness. . . .

Around eight in the morning the fish-finder bleeps. "Beep . . . beep . . . beep! Zzzzz!" My dad screams, "We're on!" as line zips out even with a 300-pound drag. "Anchor off, start the engines!"

The fish drags the line out before the engines are even started. Time goes by too fast in the moment, everything rushed, in panic, in excitement. After a long, hard fight, we realize, it's a shark. A seven-foot blue shark. A disappointment. Can't sell it. Can't eat it. Up against the boat, he breaks loose, and we reset the lines in hopes for a tuna. Washington Irving said: "There is certainly something in angling that tends to produce a serenity of the mind."

So true, even when the "big one" gets away or isn't the big one you want.

Hunter kept insisting he could not draw, but he tried a watercolor wash, colors dropped on clear water on watercolor paper, and was happy with how it looked. Just touching a brush with color on it to clear water lets the colors run the way they do in the natural world—for sky, plants, trees, leaves, lakes, oceans, sunrise, sunset—anything in nature.

Torn paper, which he did to illustrate "For Bow Hunters Only," also worked for him when he became frustrated with drawing. Both illustration techniques are relatively easy and yet quite effective in enhancing each particular poem.

To illustrate "Fight of a Buffalo with Wolves" he used photographs he had taken of the buffalo calf they rescued from the field.

In his last double-page spread of the year, he had the confidence to try sketching—the boat they use for tuna fishing. He spread it across the two pages in the Heart Book and felt comfortable with what he had drawn.

Particularly noteworthy in his case, his writing and his confidence in writing improved dramatically as he read poetry and constructed his Heart Book.

Caden S.

DESCRIPTION OF HEART MAP

THOUGHTS ON POETRY

RESPONSE TO POETS: **Heaney, Dickinson, St. Vincent Millay**

WHAT I NOTICED ABOUT CADEN'S RESPONSES

Encasing the whole heart is the winding trail of pale purple yarn, twisting and turning around it and creating different sections. If followed, the yarn leads back around and to the top of the heart where my mischievous cat plays with it. I chose to do this because of my love for my cat, Frodo, who greets me every day when I come home from school by climbing onto my shoulders while purring loudly. I chose to create the opening at the top to show that I have an "open heart" and was accepting and welcoming, not closed off to new ideas and experiences.

Bursting out of the top of the heart is an astronaut, representing one of my favorite books, *The Martian*. The spaceman also represents my curiosity towards outer space, not just the stars and planets, but the mystery that lies beyond the telescope's view. I never did want to become an astronaut, but I did always wonder what zero gravity felt like. It would also be cool to design rockets and rovers.

Caden S. Heart Map

Instead of wishing to travel space, I took a liking to what we have here on Earth. The airplane represents travel. Ever since the long road trip that started with my family in 2008, I have loved traveling and exploring the wonders of each place. I hope to travel even more: to shield my eyes from the glare of the hot sand as I look up at the Pyramids of Gaza, take a ride on the Autobahn, and climb Mount Roraima, peering over the sheer drop and feeling my stomach drop at the thought of falling, before slowly backing away terrified.

The two masks represent ancient Greek Muses, Thalia and Melpomene (comedy and tragedy). Theater is one of my passions. . . . In theater you are able to become the character you are cast as, becoming one with them. In doing this you boost your ability to understand those around you and how they feel. Acting not only develops social skills, but helps you make others happy.

The book shows my readiness to learn and my love of reading. On rainy days I love getting lost in a good book, the ones that drown out everything around you and suck you into the world between the pages.

The cardboard box holds a baseball bat, a soccer ball and a football. I love sports, especially the thrill of sliding into second, snatching a puck out of the air, or heading a soccer ball past the goalie and into the net. I don't play football, but I like a good game of football with my friends, or with my dad and brothers.

What is more beautiful than a sunset on the beach?

The tree stands rooted to convey my will to preserve nature. Mankind has been hacking away at wildlife to create cities with skyscrapers and other unrestrained development in the name of "progress." My brothers once called me a tree hugger and the animal whisperer for my love of nature. One day I wish that the human race will pay full attention to Earth and shift its focus on how to preserve it for future generations.

Favorites: Summer. Spending time at any lake in NH, tubing and waterskiing with my family. Ben and Jerry's ice cream. My brother Lucas's popcorn. And spike ball with my two brothers. Diving. Spiking. Last second passes. All year I wait for summer.

Poetry . . . means stories of beauty, stories of anguish, or calm times of peace. When I hear the word, I think of a rhythm printed onto a page, one that calms you and tells you something in a secretive way. I think of the Robert Frost poem "Stopping by Woods on a Snowy Evening" [*You Come Too* 1975]: second grade, the whole class sitting on the carpeted floor in a circle, the teacher reading, and several classmates arguing over who got to sit next to the teacher.

I think of first grade: Shel Silverstein's [1974] *Where the Sidewalk Ends*, the poem "Boa Constrictor" and the class laughing and loving the way the teacher always read the last line. I think "Carrots" and how I cringed when I looked at the drawing, feeling bad for the boy. Poetry is images that pop into my head like a kaleidoscope.

Poetry is different in its secretive way of conveying a story. The meaning of a poem is different to every person and does not tell the reader what to feel . . . it is astonishing to recognize the stealthy way a poem wriggles its way into your mind and creates emotions while nudging your consciousness. When you read a poem you are embraced by the rhythm. You feel a sense of peace and safety when you read a well-crafted poem, as if every word has been carefully vetted and strung together just so.

My favorite poet is Robert Frost. I like the slow, calming way that he writes. There is always a calming feeling, like a gentle awakening . . .

"Blackberry-Picking" by Seamus Heaney
From Poems 1965–1975 (Heaney 1988)

RESPONSE: This is a poem about the end of summer for the poet, Seamus Heaney, as a young child. The child picks the first blackberries of the season and attempts to save the richness of the beginning of spring. He learns again and again each year that he could not save the berries for later. He would have needed to eat the berries early. It is a sad disappointment to realize that as Robert Frost also observed, "Nothing gold can stay" [Latham 1967]. The end of summer usually is disappointing for young children and trying to save the blackberries could represent a young boy's attempt to hold on tightly to the succulent, juicy day of summer before school begins. The optimistic hopes of a young boy crash up against the realities of nature and savoring delicious blackberries beyond the season is a child's dream that cannot be fulfilled. The line "I always felt like crying" shows that a young boy's optimism is hard to dampen, and that life's lessons are sometimes hard to accept.

I noticed the alliteration in the poet's use of the "b" sound throughout the poem (briars, bleached our boots, blobs burned, . . .), a sound that connects to the word blackberry. I also noticed the "b" sound is a harder consonant, perhaps because disappointment is harsh, a life reality. I also notice the tranquil, smooth rhythm of the poem. Each line has ten syllables.

I wondered why the poet chose the reference to Bluebeard, a man who murdered his wives and had sticky blood left on his hands, into a poem about disappointment. I wonder if the blackberry juice is symbolic for blood. I

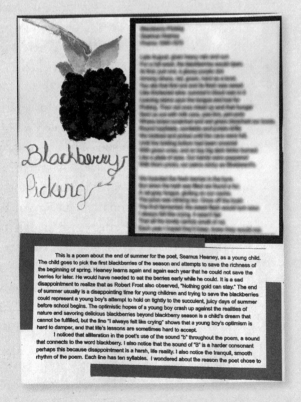

also wonder if picking a fruit has a biblical connection to picking an apple in the Garden of Eden because I know the poet grew up attending Catholic schools. In addition, I notice that the poem does not quite rhyme. There are only four true rhymes: clots/knots, rot/not. I think that it is significant that he chose to rhyme these four words.

This poem reminded me of the way that I would try to save my candy from Christmas, Halloween and Easter, so that I could savor and prolong the feeling of happiness the candy represents. I didn't realize that the chocolate would go white or the taffy dry out.

The poem also reminded me of when my family and I would pick blueberries at Mendum's Pond after a long day of kayaking. Gathering them in a large water thermos, each juicy orb made a soft thumping sound as we plopped them in. . . . At the end of our adventure "our palms (were) sticky as Bluebeard's."

"There Is No Frigate Like a Book" by Emily Dickinson

From Poetry for Young People: Emily Dickinson *(Bolin 1994)*

RESPONSE: This poem supports my idea that books take you far away without you ever needing to move. You can be transported to a magical land with dragons, or be stuck on a boat in the Arctic. Where it takes you is unique in imagery to you, because everybody creates the images in a different way. It is special to read a book because nothing else can do what they do. Nothing else can turn something so bland, like a black and white page, into a grand adventure in a second. Reading forces you to create your own landscape from the words given to you. When someone reads the word "mountain," a myriad of images pop into their head that are all unique to them. When watching a movie they are given every detail of the scene with no room for imagination. That's one reason why books are greater learning tools than movies.

The poem says that no boat can take you as far and as fast as a book can, and no horse can explore as much as you can from one page of poetry. Even the poorest can travel using a book, for it is the cheapest of travels. I like this statement. As a traveler I am always looking for the next chance I get to travel and reading books turns out to be the most readily available opportunity.

"First Fig" by Edna St. Vincent Millay

From Poetry for Young People: Edna St. Vincent Millay
(Schoonmaker 1999)

RESPONSE: I chose this poem because I was amazed at how many meanings it can have in only four lines. It could be about living in the moment, putting aside your differences and sharing something with everybody, about how you don't need money to find joy, or it could simply be about a poet watching a candle burn. I believe that one of the biggest ideas of the poem is living in the moment and savoring what you have. The author enjoys the beauty of the candle while it lasts and doesn't worry about it dying out.

. . . Every other line rhymes. The rhyming words (ends/friends, night/light) cause a bouncing rhythm by starting with a soft and low-sounding word and then using a sharp and high-pitched sounding word. It reminded me of a bouncing ball and is playful in the same way. I think Millay did this to make the reader experience the poem as upbeat, instead of mistaking it for something sad. . . . The fact that she calls her own light lovely shows that she has a lot of confidence in herself.

This poem reminds me of the snowy night when the power goes out and we light candles. . . . On these nights we play board games. The darkness broken by the candlelight keeps everybody's attention on the game. Those nights are amazing because we get the chance to think, and be more fully present, in our screen-packed lives.

My candle burns at both ends;
It will not last the night;
But ah, my foes, and oh, my friends—
It gives a lovely light!

"First Fig" by Edna St. Vincent Millay
From Great Short Poems

Caden is meticulous and intentional in his reading of these poems. He chose challenging poems and worked hard rereading them for their formatting, word choice, conveyed feelings, imagery, and connections to him. He revised his reading as thoroughly as he revisited and often revised his writing. He read the following poems, choosing a range of poets he did not know but wanted to know because of peer recommendations as they discovered new poets. He is also so thoughtful and thorough in his description of what is on his Heart Map and why, as well as his knowledge of poetry and where that comes from.

Lucas S.

To be honest, I've never really liked reading or writing poetry. Whenever I hear the word "poetry" I think of metaphoric riddles, similes and personification. . . . One of the reasons I like poetry is because there is a lot of white space on the page and, therefore, quicker to read.

Poetry is different from other kinds of writing in that the poet is allowed to use fragments of sentences and the message isn't as clear as in prose. The readers can have different ideas about what the poem is saying, and they both could be right.

I like Robert Frost because some of the first poems that I read were by him. I like that he is a poet from New Hampshire and that his poem "Nothing Gold Can Stay" was in *The Outsiders* [Hinton 1967].

"Out, Out—" by Robert Frost

From Poetry for Young People: Robert Frost *(Schmidt 1994)*

RESPONSE: I chose "Out, Out—" because it was the first poem I read around a Harkness table when I shadowed my older brother. This is a disturbing poem about a young boy who, "doing a man's work," tragically dies after an accident while cutting wood. Robert Frost uses vivid imagery when he describes the setting: "The buzz saw snarled and rattled in the yard/And made dust and dropped stove-length sticks of wood/Sweet-scented stuff when the breeze drew across it." . . . The poem seems like nothing out of the ordinary at first, just a regular day cutting wood. But just like that, a simple distraction, the single word "Supper," leads to a tragic event. There is an ominous tone to the poem with the repetition of the phrase "snarled and rattled" in the lines "And the saw snarled and rattled, snarled and rattled/As it ran light, or had to bear a load." The title "Out, Out—" reminds me of Macbeth. When he learns that his wife has died, he says, "Out, out, brief candle!" Both of these are tragedies. Like in Macbeth, when the boy dies, the others around him can't do anything to change the outcome of the event, so they "turned to their affairs."

Lucas drew a small boy, trying to convey the childlike innocence of this boy doing a man's work. In the boy's stance, almost a shrug, he shows the acceptance of this—it is the way life is. The boy did not want to lose his hand. "Don't let him cut my hand off/The doctor, when he comes. Don't let him, sister!" But the boy loses more than his hand: "the watcher at his pulse took fright/No one believed. They listened at his heart/Little—less—nothing!—and that ended it/No more to build on there." Harsh words from Frost, but conveying the fact that life is hard. We go on.

With the intention of reflecting the poem, Lucas chose the following quotes from Frost:

> **"Poetry is a way of taking life by the throat."**

> **"To be a poet is a condition, not a profession."**

> **"A poem begins as a lump in the throat, a sense of wrong, a homesickness, a lovesickness."**

"Travel" by Edna St. Vincent Millay

From Poetry for Young People: Edna St. Vincent Millay
(Schoonmaker 1999)

RESPONSE: I chose this poem because I love to travel. Millay captures and describes her feelings and her surroundings. She hears the distant sound of a train and can see its cinders in the sky. She implies that she likes where she is and her surroundings. "My heart is warm with the friends I make." However, she says that she'd take any train no matter where it goes. She'd leave all behind to jump on a train that is going somewhere, anywhere new. I, too, have this wanderlust, this deep desire to soak in new places and people. Snapshots of unknown places, and landscapes ignite an inner spark within me and make my heart beat just a little bit faster.

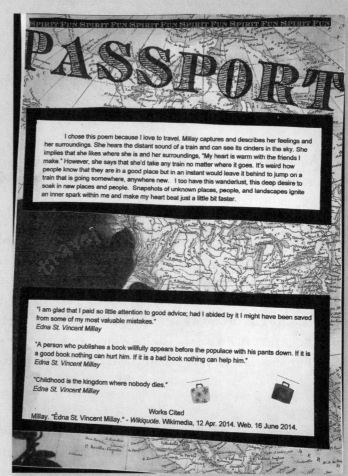

Lucas never felt comfortable drawing. Notice in this illustration he found a map that worked well as a background for his double-page spread. Simple, but intentional and effective as it related to him and Millay's poem.

In Millay's words: "I am glad that I paid so little attention to good advice; had I abided by it, I might have been saved from some of my most valuable mistakes."

Maria S.

On my heart map, I have three life-changing moments, three younger siblings: Anya, Eli, and Max. They mean the world to me. I have been through the best and the worst with them. My older sister is also there. Just seeing her reminds me of all the wonderful times we had together. Racing in Mario Kart, arguing over who is the worse cook. We all argue and make everything a competition, but when even one sibling is missing, the house feels empty.

I also have a huge wave accompanied by swim goggles and a water bottle. I am passionate for swimming, and have been swimming competitively since I was seven years old.

On my heart map I also have a Russian flag. Both of my parents and my older sister were born in Russia. My first language was Russian, and I still speak it quite fluently. All of my extended family lives in Russia. At most, I see my grandparents once a year.

Maria S. Heart Map

Lastly Cape Cod, known for its beaches, lighthouses, and the call of seagulls. My family's favorite place.

When I hear the word *poetry*, I think *school*. But, that aside, limericks and nursery rhymes jump inside my head. I also think of rhyming and rhythm. I also think sunflowers, for one of the first poems that I wrote in grade school was about sunflowers.

Poetry can be interpreted many different ways. It also tends to have some sort of music or rhythm-like feel to it.

I don't really like poetry, or know any poets.

"The Rose Family" by Robert Frost

From You Come Too *(Frost 1975)*

RESPONSE: I have always disliked poetry. Everything about it. I couldn't understand the deeper meaning nor the story behind every word. To me poetry didn't tell a story but how could it be writing if it didn't tell a story? Well, "The Rose Family" is the first poem I actually enjoyed reading. I can sense that there is something behind those words, hiding. This poem flows and rhymes. It seems simple and ordinary. It calls out to humanity in a loving, yet eerie way.

This poem almost suggests that everything is the same and more things are becoming less unique and more generic. You could also view this as everyone is beautiful, like a rose. That connection reached out to me the most. It made me feel beautiful, a feeling that very few things make me experience.

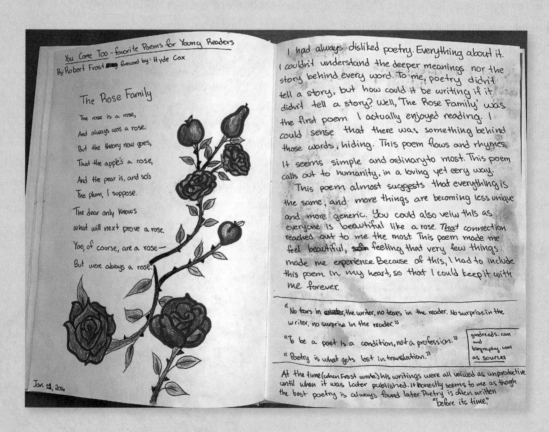

"Someone" by Abigail Lynne Becker

From A Box of Rain (Becker 1993)

RESPONSE: This poem is about trying to find one's place. A place in the crowd, in the world, a place that is yours. And only yours. I could almost connect with this poem on a spiritual level. In fact, I am also, looking for my place.

What is your role in the world? Ever since I was a child, I never fit in quite right. I wasn't a popular kid, nor a nerd, nor a loner. Even today I wonder where I might be located in the social world. *What will you be when you grow up? What do you want to do?* These are questions that have haunted me since kindergarten. I have no idea. Should I be a baker? An artist? A mathematician? All things I am okay at, but I have never excelled in anything. I was always unsure of what exactly I wanted to do in this world, and where I would belong.

Did you hear? I heard she's moving again. I heard these things around me my whole life, and it always made me question, did I really have friends? Constantly moving, changing schools, I never found the time for strong bonds, deep friendships. Most that were headed in that direction were broken off whenever my dad suddenly changed jobs. I never had someone "who wants to come along," someone who would jump off a bridge if I did. Not until recently at least.

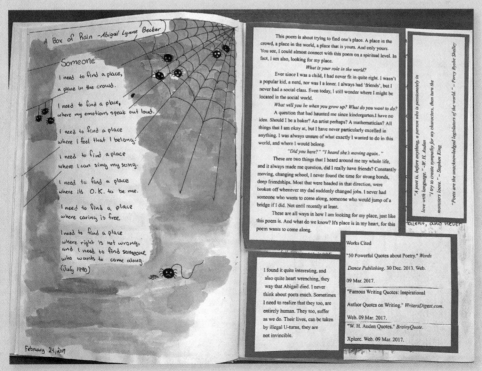

Watercolor illustration

"silence, my friend." by r. h. Sin

From Whiskey Words & a Shovel II *(Sin 2016)*

RESPONSE: Thousands of people remain silent in the worst situations: during a life-changing argument, when they are feeling ill, when someone is attempting to assault them. The abused are often silent, and so are the mentally ill. So many people's lives are thrown around and torn apart because of silence. Too many people consider "silence their best friend," and so many sacrifices are made just to save their friendship with silence.

When friends are hurting or you are hurting, one rarely speaks out. It is saddening the number of lives gone to waste for the lack of noise. We need to speak up more often.

I had a friend in fifth grade who started making jokes that put me down. . . . I hated it. After more than a year, I finally spoke and now the two of us are good friends, sharing food, sleeping in each other's beds, and eating each other's macaroni and cheese.

People should speak more. The way we are now, we will all end up like withered flowers that never got a chance to bloom.

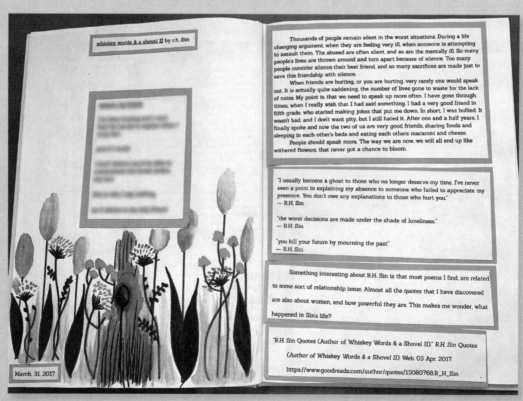

Watercolor illustration

"Why Nobody Pets the Lion at the Zoo"
by John Ciardi

From Reflections on a Gift of Watermelon Pickle
(Dunning, Lueders, and Smith 1966)

RESPONSE: The rhyming in this poem and the two lines per stanza make it fun to read and easy to remember. (It seems like a light-hearted poem.)

The truth in this poem is that many people, and animals, often have a heart of gold or kindness, but have something preventing them from showing it. (The lion "just can't trust his teeth.") People especially, who have been through tough times or seen something particularly terrifying, have things (many even a condition like PTSD) that make it hard for them to cope and we don't see it on the outside.

As an eight-year-old having gone to the zoo several times, I often wondered, "Why can't we pet the lions? They look so fluffy and nice." I had no idea they could bite.

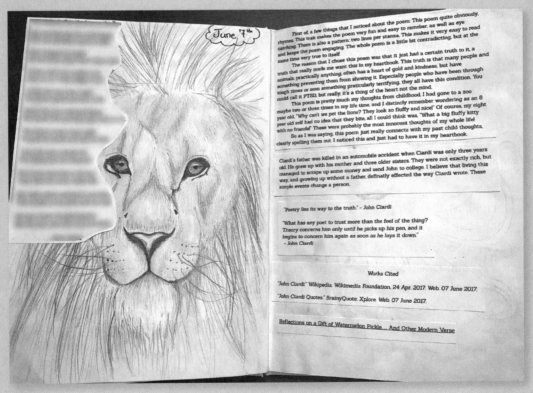

Pencil Sketch

"Once by the Pacific" by Robert Frost

From The Poetry of Robert Frost *(Latham 1967)*

Watercolor and Zentangle

Now when I hear the word *poetry* I think about movement and feeling. Is that odd? School will ALWAYS come to mind when I hear the word *poetry*, but it is no longer associated with negative feelings.

Poetry is more of an art form, and has no rules. It can be short, long, abrupt, soothing. It can be viewed and interpreted in many different ways.

I think my favorite poet is Robert Frost. His poems almost have a watery feel to them, smooth and no rough edges. I don't know why, but poems by Frost just tend to pull me in and hold me there.

Joshua T.

THOUGHTS ON POETRY (BEFORE AND AFTER HEART BOOK)
RESPONSE TO POETS: Stafford, Herford, Soto

What mainly comes to mind with poetry is a form of writing which is set apart from all other forms, in the sense that poetry evokes more emotion, depth, and power than any other.

Poetry is like a song without the instruments. It has a rhythm, a specific format, and it's one of the forms of writing which holds the most emotion.

Poetry is as close to pure art as it can get. I think of people's emotions and ideas, transcended into words.

Poetry is different from other kinds of writing in that it requires more thinking from the reader, and is open for individual interpretations. It's emotion which has found words.

I like William Shakespeare and Gary Soto, mainly because of the deeper message that they convey through their writing, especially Shakespeare, who discusses humanity and other morals.

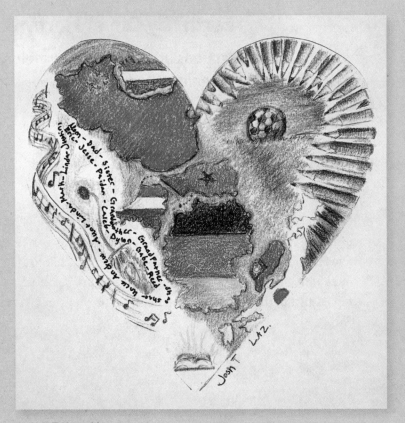

Joshua T. Heart Map

"The Day Millicent Found the World"
by William Stafford

From The Way It Is *(Stafford 1998)*

RESPONSE: What I mainly noticed about this poem is that it tells the story about a girl discovering nature and the world. I can personally relate to that because I remember when I was younger I would sometimes go out into the woods and simply sit in the middle of the trees. I remember the warm sun beaming down and I just sat there and drew everything I saw. For me, Millicent is me.

When I read the poem, she embodies my own curiosity, and natural affinity to nature.

"Earth" by Oliver Herford

From Reflections on a Gift of Watermelon Pickle
(Dunning, Lueders, Smith 1966)

RESPONSE: This poem seems to nudge at the notion of Earth and its inhabitants being so insignificant and little, to the point where we're nothing more than a shooting star to a kid ("from a distant planet") who watches as we "fall through space in a hissing, headlong flight" into the sun. To me, I find it incredibly humbling, and quite scary, at how miniscule we are compared to the universe. What I love is how Herford grouped all the organisms up as one, philosophers with ants and lice, men and maggots, all in one, which implies that in the end, it won't matter what or who you are.

"The Philosophy of Dog and Man" by Gary Soto
From Who Will Know Us? *(Soto 1990)*

RESPONSE: This poem caught my eye, and my heart, when I read it. I chose it for how much optimism the dog has. It was saddening reading about a stray dog that just wants food, has a broken or injured foot and is in the rain. But it was also inspirational. I wish I could be like that dog, happy, no matter how tough things get. I guess the man can't comprehend how the dog can be happy; even I can't understand it.

Max T.

ARTISTRY OF HEART MAP

LAYOUT OF DOUBLE-PAGE SPREAD

RESPONSE TO POETS: Sandburg, Cooper, Baker, Walker

ART INVITATION: Zentangle

WHAT I NOTICED ABOUT MAX'S THOUGHTFULNESS AS A READER AND ARTIST

Max did everything with great care and intention, taking advantage of every learning opportunity. If you look carefully at his Heart Map you can see how serious he is even as a fourteen-year-old, thinking about a future in either marine biology or prosthetics engineering, and valuing the qualities of confidence, intelligence, control, patience, and perseverance in his life.

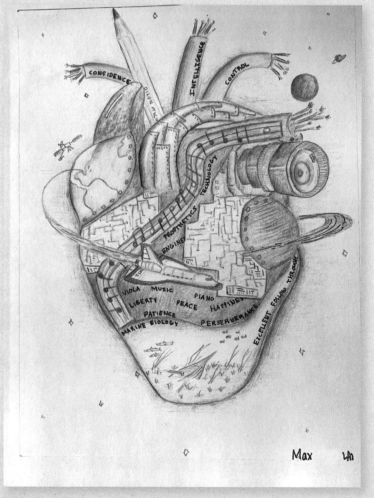

Max T. Heart Map

From Poetry for Young People: Carl Sandburg (Bolin 1995)

Each double-page spread was done as carefully as the one focused on Carl Sandburg's "Under a Telephone Pole."

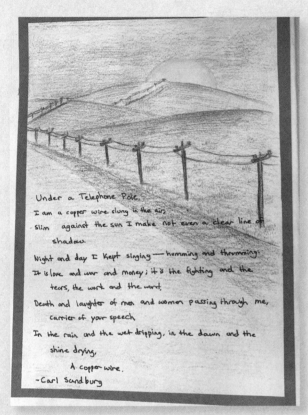

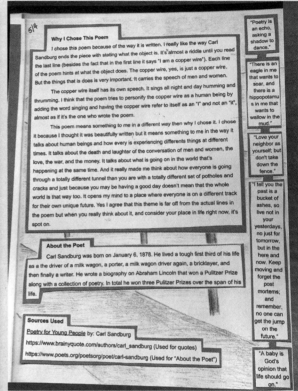

"Mars Poetica" by Wyn Cooper

From Mars Poetica

Imagine you're on
Mars, looking at earth,
a swirl of colors in
the distance.
Tell me what you miss
most, or least.
Let your feelings
rise to the surface.
Skim that surface
with a tiny net.
Now you're getting
the hang of it.

Tell us your story
slantwise, streetwise,
in the disguise of an
astronaut in his suit.
Tell us something we
didn't know before:
how words mean things
we didn't know we
knew.

RESPONSE: I chose this poem because I'm interested in space. I've watched every space documentary on Netflix and I still can't get enough of it. Even though I would never strive to be an astronaut, I still have a passion for space exploration. I was looking for a poem that wasn't just about space, because then this writing would be more like a lecture. I was looking for a poem that doesn't just explain the objects in space, but the emotions you would feel if you were in space.

This poem tells you to imagine yourself on Mars, looking at Earth from a different perspective. It tells you to catch your feelings with a net and make it into a story. It asks you to tell that story with different perspectives: "slantwise, streetwise, and in the disguise of an astronaut in his suit." Slantwise and streetwise I could understand, but the disguise of an astronaut in his suit really made me think. Does it mean to tell your story from the perspective of an astronaut on the moon or as a new astronaut on a new planet?

I think that it's from the perspective of a new astronaut on Mars because the last lines are asking to tell Earth something new, something they didn't know. How words mean things we didn't know we knew. This makes sense because the new astronaut would be seeing things in a way that no one has ever seen before. And they would be feeling things that they never felt before.

Maybe I should rethink dreaming on becoming an astronaut; it doesn't sound half bad.

"The Sea" by David Baker

From poets.org

RESPONSE: I chose this poem because of my curiosity for the deep ocean. It still amazes me that we have only explored 5% of the ocean, which covers 71% of the earth's surface. I love watching documentaries, especially ocean ones. I think the reason why I'm interested in the ocean (and space) is because I like to explore. I think it's so cool to discover new things that nobody has ever seen before.

This poem, with its lines, "sea urchins spread . . . to quiver their hundred-plus spines . . ." reminds me of when I went to Hawaii last summer. The only way to get out of the coral reel was to walk over a bed of sea urchins. My dad and I didn't realize it though until it was too late. . . . I didn't wear shoes so my feet were bleeding because of the urchins. My dad was smart and wore shoes and coaxed me to keep coming. After the excursion, my feet were purple and green because of the spikes of the sea urchins.

"When You See Water" by Alice Walker

From https://poeticous.com

RESPONSE: I think the main idea of this poem is that nobody belongs to anyone. The water, in the poem, is its own self. Yes, it is located in certain places, like the ocean or the river, but it is not the river. I don't belong to a specific person or a specific location. I am my own self, just like the water.

Walker also wrote *The Color Purple*[Walker 1982], one of my favorite books. I think the main idea in this poem, we are our own selves, is also the main idea in the novel, we are our own selves.

Zentangle

Sophie W.

"A Passing Glimpse" by Robert Frost

From You Come Too *(Frost 1975)*

I often see flowers from a passing car
That are gone before I can tell what they are.

I want to get out of the train and go back
To see what they were beside the track.

I name all the flowers I am sure they weren't:
Not fireweed loving where woods have burnt—

Not bluebells gracing a tunnel mouth—
Not lupine living on sand and drouth.

Was something brushed across my mind
That no one on earth will ever find?

Heaven gives its glimpses only to those
Not in position to look too close.

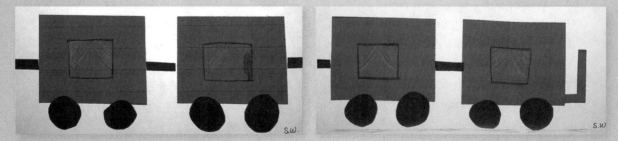

Illustrated response (cut paper) to "A Passing Glimpse" by Robert Frost

RESPONSE: When I read this poem, I knew it was the one I wanted to learn more about. It took me to places of imagination and mystery with its rhyming lines. Frost lets his imagination run to incredible things "that no one on earth will ever find." To me, this poem is a perfect example of what poetry should be—images in your head. Like the "bluebells gracing a tunnel mouth."

Maybe Frost had something brushed across his mind that no one on earth will ever find. We only get passing glimpses IF we are not able to look too close. Heaven and poetry can keep you wondering.

"Emily Dickinson's To-Do List" by Andrea Carlisle

From The Writer's Almanac *(2010)*

RESPONSE: The main reason I chose this poem is because it is unique. How many poems do you see that are in the form of a to do list? To me, this poem also has some humor. On Monday, Tuesday, Wednesday, Thursday and Friday, the first thing on the list has to do with a white dress, or an off-white dress.

When I first read this poem, I knew exactly how I wanted to illustrate it—each day a different list and topped with a ribbon as if tied to something to remind Emily what to do. I love how in this short, brief poem I learned so much about Emily Dickinson. She was a kind of secret poet, hence all the references to hiding her poetry. She also was a kind of keep to yourself kind of person, seldom leaving her room or even her house. Instead of talking with visitors she stayed behind a door and eavesdropped on their conversations.

Sadly, only a few of her poems were published in her lifetime and publishers altered them to meet the "poetry rules" of the time. I think she was most likely an observing kind of person and speculated about the world around her.

Like so many of my students, Sophie was most uncomfortable trying to find an artistic way to illustrate the poems she chose. By suggesting she use cut paper, she came up with the idea of the train, as something we can't get off when there are so many things we pass that we would like to look at more closely. Like Frost we can only guess what we didn't see, never knowing for sure what we missed.

In the poem about Emily Dickinson she found a very simple, yet effective way to illustrate Carlisle's words in a way that mirrored the poem and Dickinson.

Before doing the Heart Book I thought that poetry was often about nature or beautiful things or ideas. I thought that poetry usually rhymed or flowed together in some sort of way. I knew that there were many different kinds and formats to poetry. Since doing the Heart Book, I have noticed that poetry can be about anything and everything. Not just beautiful things. It can be about fury, sadness, happiness, nature, that old rickety porch swing or even other people. Emily Dickinson, for example. Since doing the Heart Book I have learned that poetry should really just be your heart speaking. You should write it for you and share it with other people.

Daiyao Z.

DESCRIPTION OF HEART MAP

RESPONSE TO POETS: Becker, Baca

The sun is crucial to anyone's life. It signifies happiness, which is usually most people's ultimate goal in life. Sidewalks, stained with rain, are signs of calmness and peace to me. The sight of snow that just fell is just about the most perfect thing I can think of. It is flawless, and almost pains me to step in it.

I love to read, and can read for hours.

My life revolves around music. I have played the piano for eight years, and it is the thing that I have been committed to the longest in my life.

Family consists of the most important people in my life. They accept me for who I am in any situation, and push me to strive for my best.

Daiyao Z. Heart Map

"What would I do . . ." by Abigail Lynn Becker

From A Box of Rain (Becker 1993)

RESPONSE: This poem illustrates one of the things I most value in my life. I grew up learning that an education can open up many doors in the future. I was taught to learn as much as I can, whenever I can. The part where it says, "cries out from deep within my soul, grasping desperately for something to hold," reminds me how much I like things that are stable and never change. That is why I like math so much. There is always a definite answer to everything. When it says, "But I'll sit here in my luxury, and drink a toast to minds that are free" tells me that knowledge can set you free in the world.

Carl Sandburg said that "Poetry is the opening and closing of a door, leaving those who look through to guess about what is seen during the moment." Poetry really is about guessing what it truly means to the reader. Everyone can see something differently, and the same poem can mean something different from one person to another. Sometimes poetry is straight forward, sometimes it is not. Sometimes poetry can be a statement, clearly understood by others when they read it. It can also be a question. Poetry can be laced with happiness, and yet have depression hidden underneath all the real words. Only when someone reads the whole poem do they understand what it means to them, and yet, no one else.

What would I do if I couldn't learn?
I've got to give in to that thing that burns,
Cries out from inside my soul
Grasping desperately for something to hold

A word, a song, a silent fear
A flower, a string, a bitter tear.
These things I hold
And know as true.
I've learned how to use them
and what they do.
But still you say I've gone too far
Because I know the names of every star.
But I'll sit here in my luxury.
And drink a toast to minds that are free.
I think it's great.
You ___ say it's dumb.
Just where do you get your information from?
What makes you king of this here hill?
What kind of bird is on my window sill?
Bet you don't know that,
So step aside and throw down your hat.

Try to see what the world's got to teach
And grasp that knowledge if your hands can reach.
Hold on tight, don't let go
Just think of all the things you'll know
And maybe someday you'll get to go
Play piano, fish for bass
And name every single type of grass.
And what is it that YOU can do?
Can you pinpoint the cycles of the moon?
Or tell me the story of Daniel Boone?

No, I don't think you can.
You're just a glaring, ignorant man
{ By: Abigail Lynne Becker   A Box of Rain }

"A Daily Joy to Be Alive"
by Jimmy Santiago Baca

From Selected Poems of Jimmy Santiago Baca *(Baca 2011)*

RESPONSE: This poem really made me think about the future. Sometimes I feel like things are slipping out of reach. Like I will never achieve anything in life. I must work hard each day or else my dreams will slowly wither and die each day I wait to pursue them. . . .

I do not live in someone's footsteps. I like to admire what others have achieved, but I do not want to follow what they did, or build from their ideas. I wish to achieve something that is all my own. To do something that no one else has done.

As I descend into "unknown abysses" I still have my doubts that I will not find anything but darkness. I feel that it might be highly likely that there will not be anything that I achieve, no matter how badly I want it, so I must hang on to things that will definitely hold me. Things that I am good at. A Plan B. . . . I hope that my dreams of fire that "flicker and twist" will not burn through the rope, and make me fall.

Baca was abandoned by his parents at the age of two, and placed in an orphanage years after living with his grandmother. When he was 21 he was convicted on charges of drug possession and spent more than six years in prison. While there he taught himself to read and write, and began to compose poetry. He sold the poems to inmates in exchange for cigarettes.

I wonder if his poems became the "tree or boulder" that kept him from falling even further?

Finding Writing and Reading in Heart Maps

> If you think poetry isn't important to your students, you are not listening to them. You are not noticing the headphones in their ears, blasting poetry to soothe their walk to class. . . .
>
> Learning about poetry (how to read it, write it, and appreciate it) is an integral part of teaching students about all forms of writing. . . . Poetry, more than any other form of writing, trains students to take into account the style of language. This close looking and listening is crucial to writing well in any manner. It would be hard to say that any outstanding essay does not involve meticulous word choice or the ability to persuade a reader through sheer aesthetic prowess. Poetry teaches students how to do this.
>
> —Dorothea Lasky, "What Poetry Teaches Us About the Power of Persuasion"

Most of what Georgia Heard (1999) writes about in *Awakening the Heart* in describing the Heart Maps is focused on using them for finding ideas for writing. My students certainly use them in that way also. There are so many ways I offer students to help them find those topics that matter to them, and Heart Maps are just one of those ways. The examples I share with you here show how specifically the Heart Maps contributed to the finding of writing topics that mattered most to the kids.

I don't know for sure, but I suspect that the reading of poetry contributed to the power of their writing: precise word choice, variety in length of sentences to control pace and rhythm, vivid imagery to put the reader in the moment, and focus on an engaging topic, for the writer as well as the reader. As Lasky (2012) says, it could be "meticulous word choice" coupled with "sheer aesthetic prowess" that astutely engages and often persuades a reader to a certain stance. I see those qualities in each of the following pieces.

Kenzie B.

RESPONSE TO POETS: Becker, Stafford, Neruda, Frye

THOUGHTS ON POETRY (BEFORE AND AFTER HEART MAP)

PERSUASIVE ESSAY: "Do Music Programs Have a Purpose?" by Kenzie, Taylor, and Brady

Poetry is flowing words, strategically placed for the most powerful message. It is written to express feelings, tell stories, and give messages in a way that actually makes you search for it. It is short and sweet and gets to the point. It lays out a map for you to decode the message without having the whole story laid out in front of you. . . . It makes you think.

Ellen Hopkins is my favorite poet because her poems tell a story, which makes me really get into the poem and have a stronger connection to it.

Kenzie B. Heart Map

"Triangle of Friends" and "Farewell"
by Abigail Lynne Becker

From A Box of Rain (Becker 1993)

RESPONSE: My friends are my life. I simply couldn't live without them. They mean the world to me. Abby's poem shows that just hanging out with friends, being happy in each other's presence is what's important. The poem also taught me that as life goes on you meet new people, make new friends and expand friendships. The more people you love, the more people you trust, the more people you care for, the happier your life will be.

Abigail shows in "Farewell" that even though we lose or outgrow friends, if the time we did have with them was filled with happiness, you will always value that friendship. Even when friends move on, we should value and cherish what we had, and wish each other the best.

"Sitting Up Late" by William Stafford

From Learning to Live in the World (Stafford 1994)

RESPONSE: I was always a pretty mature, loving kid. Always had to be outside. I would pretend to be a fairy or a wizard that could control the elements of earth. As I grew up I drifted away from being that kid who is outside 24/7. Technology quickly engulfed me as soon as I hit 13ish. iPhones, laptops, tablets consumed every spare minute I had. One day I decided I needed to unplug. I sat on my best friend's roof in the middle of the night. Stars glistened, animals slept, the world turned silent and all I could hear was the two of us breathing. It was the most beautiful thing I have ever experienced.

William Stafford brought those memories back. Reminded me how beautiful nature really is. Truth be told, you will never be able to experience what I did that night through your iPhone screen. Your phone only makes it an idea. When you really see it, it becomes real. Animals, the stars, moon, sun, leaves, flowers, vegetables and fruits. A phone doesn't show the true beauty of nature. You have to get out there and see if for yourself. Thank you, William Stafford. I may have forgotten this all together if it wasn't for you.

In William Stafford's words:

"What you have to do as a writer is, write day in and day out
  no matter what happens."

"Lower your standards and keep writing."

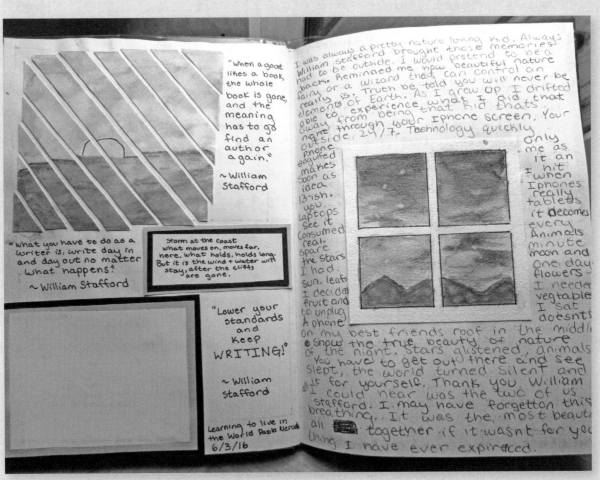

Kenzie's double-page spread to Stafford's "Staying Up Late"

"If You Forget Me" by Pablo Neruda

From https://Allpoetry.com

RESPONSE: Being forgotten. One of my biggest fears, whether it is my friends or loved ones who move on. It scares me. People leave when they find something new, something better. I don't want to be replaceable. I want to know there's someone out there that can't live without me. Misses me when I'm gone and always remembers where I am. I always thought any friend would be a friend forever. But I realize that friends come and go. They move on, find better, newer things to fill their lives. I'm forgotten again.

Neruda showed me that being forgotten isn't as bad as it seems. Neruda showed me that you just have to move on. It might be hard, especially if it's someone you love or a friend you think you can't live without. Move on. If you live in the past you can't create the future. You have to move on, the way they did. They found something better, something new. Who says you won't also? Just because you're somebody's old friend or lover doesn't mean you can't be someone's new one, too.

"Do Not Stand at My Grave and Weep" by Mary Elizabeth Frye

From https://Yourdailypoem.com

RESPONSE: This poem reminded me of my grandparents. All of their deaths were traumatic. My papa, Ronald Boyd, died of throat cancer when I was eight. My other papa, Donald Bruhm, choked and had a heart attack at a Christmas party, where I watched him helplessly. I was eleven years old and we were the best of friends. You can't imagine what it's like watching your grandfather die in front of you, and no one can help.

A year later, my Nannie died of lung cancer. She struggled. She couldn't walk on her own. She couldn't do simple tasks on her own. She couldn't even breathe on her own. When she died I don't even think she knew who I was.

This poem tries to make me feel better, that they are with me, guiding me along in spirit in all the quiet moments we often miss.

In the words of Winnie-the-Pooh: "How lucky I am to have someone that makes saying goodbye so hard." (Pintarest.com)

Poetry now makes me think of a short piece written to make you think about the message and how it connects to you. Poetry shows you meaning but it's up to you to take it further than what's written on the page.

Poetry takes big ideas, key words, and strong vocabulary to make an impactful piece of writing. Poetry is different because you don't need pages and pages of writing to communicate your message to others. Poetry also makes it possible for everyone to connect to it because it can be perceived in different ways, instead of one message not everyone can connect to. Poetry gives meaning to anyone who reads it.

My favorite poets are now Abigail Becker and Pablo Neruda. I found it easy to connect to their poems.

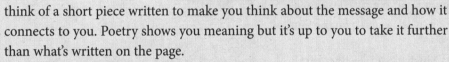

Although Kenzie's Heart Map is the only one shown here, Taylor M. and Brady M. also cited music as central and important in their lives. Heart Maps are not only for finding poetry that mattered to them; topics for writing (in the way Georgia Heard developed and uses them) also grew from the crafting of the Heart Maps. In this case the three girls collaborated on a video they produced as a culmination of our study of persuasive writing (research, political cartoons, persuasive essays, script writing, and video). The following is the script they wrote for the video.

So often in real life, writers collaborate on projects. Encouraging our students to work together and present their thinking in a variety of genres teaches them real-world skills.

Do Music Programs Have a Purpose?

The cello. The sound is breathtaking. The first time I heard it some feeling welled up inside of my chest that I couldn't even explain. Low deep notes to high notes. I loved it all, every piece of music it was used for. It didn't matter because I loved the sound. Music found me and I'm glad it did because nothing can compare to it. It lets me express myself in ways that words wouldn't. Music allows me to be me.

This is why I believe every school should offer their students a music program. Music has aspects of language, reading, math, memorization, and imagination. Music helps children and adolescents improve academically and rapidly progress their skills as time goes on.

Math: Learning to read music and understand concepts, such as time, rhythm, and pitch, connect directly to the child's math skills. Studies show (*Velasco 2012*) that children that have been learning to play instruments excel more greatly and at a more rapid pace compared to the children that don't. These children also scored higher on tests and on their overall grade for the math class and feel less of the stress of a non-instrument-playing student.

Memorization: Music promotes fast thinking, better predictions, and memorization. Lyrics and sheet music can cause children to excel in reading way beyond what is expected. The changes in keys and notes help children think ahead of what they're playing and predict what should happen in the measure of music, developing prediction skills and memorization. In music, fast thinking is key. The changes in emotion throughout the song vary in how they're played. Musicians must plan ahead so they always know what's expected and never be caught off-guard. These skills, developed by playing an instrument, will not only help them in music but will help them in everyday tasks throughout their life.

Reading: Learning music and studying lyrics can teach the student syllabification, phonics, vocabulary, and imagery. Even though it doesn't look like it, sheet music is actually reading. Each note on the staff has a corresponding letter which can be identified when playing music. Learning music alters the brain, making it easier for a child to retain and understand different sounds and words that they hear. This causes their vocabularies to be larger because they remember more things that they have heard than the child that does not play an instrument. These children perform better on vocabulary-based tests than kids who haven't learned music.

Language: Music will help a child learn a language faster. The different beats and instruments and words tell the brain this is something it wants to remember. This ability will help the child not only learn a language faster but enjoy learning it as well.

Imagination: As you know there are so many academic-based abilities that music improves. But imagination? That, too. Children that grow up with music have better imaginations because they can explore different sounds and rhythms with their instruments, encouraging them to stray from the "normal" path, and make something their own.

Life Skills: Music teaches children the importance of hard work, practice and, discipline. This is because playing an instrument isn't as easy as it looks. It takes a lot of work to get it perfect and there's always something that can be improved. Determination is what it teaches you, which is why musicians always push beyond the limits and create the impossible.

All these benefits—and not to mention the thrill of learning music. That is why we believe every student should be offered the chance to learn such an amazing thing. Music sets them up for the future and opens up endless possibilities.

"Music can name the unnamable and communicate the unknowable."

—*Leonard Bernstein*

Works Cited

Pogrebin, Robin. "Book Tackles Old Debate: Role of Art in Schools." *The New York Times.* 03 Aug. 2007. Web. 29 Mar. 2016.

Velasco, Jessica. "How the Arts Can Help Students Excel." Scientific Learning. N.p., 10 Dec. 2012. Web. 29 Mar. 2016.

Katya E.

RESPONSE TO POETS: Neruda, Oliver, Crawford

ART INVITATION: watercolor

THOUGHTS ON POETRY

POEM: "Honesty" by Katya E.

I started with the horses to form my heart. Horses have shaped my life in so many ways and are one of the most important parts of my life—whether it is riding, taking care of them (or them taking care of me) or trying to understand the way they think. Horses, both my own and others, have taught me, so much about love that it is only fitting for them to be the first thing you see in my heart.

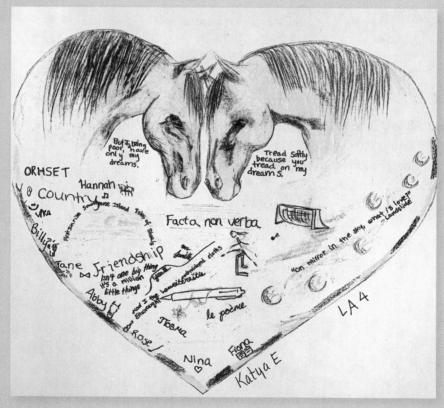

Katya E. Heart Map

I drew a pen with a flower wrapped around it, to show my love of writing. Next to it I wrote 1.5 lines from Yeats's: "He wishes for the Cloths of Heaven," and I also wrote the last two lines from that poem next to the horses. Writing is my personal therapy and my notebook is the single most distracting thing while I'm doing my homework.

I wrote the names of six of my close friends because they are the ones who support me, care about me, and with whom I love to have fun. I also wrote the names of my two horses because they, too, are friends.

When I hear the word "poetry" a feeling of safety, of belonging, and then a rush of all the emotions I have put into my own poems comes over me. It's over-whelming. I see a river, a river in my heart, because poetry flows and connects us and draws us together. Or apart. Poetry is powerful like that. That's why I love it. I think of shaping words like pottery on a wheel, spinning and spinning and remolding it with care and love, and maybe tears.

With poetry you start with an emotion. You don't need characters or a plot line or an ending. You don't need structure. It's liberating. Our stories in life, the ones we've been living, aren't over yet with poetry. Like life, you don't have to write the end. Poetry is a continuum. It bends and circles and moves in the deep-est parts of you, but never really ending.

One of my favorite poets is William Butler Yeats. I haven't read much of his work, but I am stuck on "He Wishes for the Cloths of Heaven." I love how simple it is, but how much feeling there is in every word. The words are heavy with emo-tion, but light because of the way he ties them together. Poetry is like music, and good poetry moves like music, or like a dance. Careful, gentle steps, but you feel every one.

"Poetry" by Pablo Neruda

From The Essential Neruda Selected Poems *(Neruda 2004)*

RESPONSE: I chose this poem because it describes exactly how I feel about poetry and writing poetry, and mirrors the importance of writing in my life. What struck me most at first were the first few lines: I don't know where poetry has come from in my life, or why it has come for me—only that I didn't go out looking for it. I just began to write. And writing poetry has opened so much in my mind—to the point where I could spend hours just thinking and writing, and wanting nothing else.

I love the feeling of solitariness, of seeing beautiful, haunting things within my own mind, and being able to recreate them on paper, so that someone else can feel what I feel. Poetry, for me, is all about emo-tion. When I write a poem I want someone else to feel that emotion or emotions I have tried so hard to convey through metaphors and hidden mean-ings and beautiful words. The best part, though, is the discovery—the startling realization—that when you write, you create, and when you create, you feel, and when you feel, you live. That's what Neruda was writing about in "Poetry."

To me, the last line, is the most meaningful, poignant, and moving line. It shows just how freeing writing, and especially poetry, is, and gives such a strong feeling of escaping from the dull constraints of a life without writing, without words. . . . I love the freedom, the vast emptiness of a page waiting to be filled, the knowledge that I can fill it with my words. . . .

"Poppies" by Mary Oliver

From New and Selected Poems *(Oliver 1992)*

RESPONSE: I chose this poem first for the imagery, then for the emotion, and finally for the metaphor. I love the words Mary Oliver uses—"levitation," "indigoes of darkness," "palpable and redemptive," . . . These are carefully chosen words, placed in a way to deepen and strengthen the poem. The feelings through the poem are also strong and meaningful—moving from peace and contentedness to hope to a brief period of sadness, back to hope, and lastly, a sort of triumph.

If the poppies are a metaphor for anything else, I think that what they represent can vary based on how the reader perceives it. I can see the poppies as a symbol of happiness, but even more so, I see them as those select, special people who truly enrich your life. Those rare and wonderful friends who are the brightness in the dark, the poppies in the field.

For me, two of those people came into my life two summers ago, when I was very aware of the fact that the world can be dark. I met Nina and Vika at camp (my first year) after involuntarily "growing apart" from my lifelong best friend, which was extremely painful for me. I didn't see the lesson then. I saw the inevitable darkness of my friend, whom I had loved, abandoning me. I was afraid to make more friends, afraid that I'd just be hurt again. But Nina and Vika completely embraced my virtues and my flaws, loved (still love) me for who I am. I found that I could have so much fun with them, without *ever* feeling like they were judging me or would rather be with someone else.

In this way, they are the poppies standing out, bright and strong, in the dull fields of all the people I know who don't care about me in such a deep and unconditional way. Happiness is not possible alone. Happiness is something that, when shared, grows and blossoms, like a poppy.

Katya is one of the few students I've encountered in eighth grade who has read poetry on her own and written it for many years. Because of her practice of reading and writing it, she brings a sophisticated, well-developed understanding of so much that poetry is able to do. She is delighted to read Mary Oliver and Pablo Neruda, often emailing me the poems she has newly discovered. In her responses to the poems she has chosen, she truly sees and takes to heart the intentions of the poet, yet knows how to connect the feelings so personally to herself.

Shortly after entering ninth grade at Portsmouth Christian Academy, she sent me her poem "Honesty," that she said came from her Heart Map and Heart Book. I encourage students to save their Heart Books, portfolios, and notebooks, citing their value in the future.

"Failure" by Robert Crawford

RESPONSE: I chose this poem because I know I can be too much of a perfectionist, I know that I fear failure too much, and that I need to be able to accept my own imperfections. I understand all of this, but it is not easy for me to do something—or perhaps do nothing—about it. I spend hours and hours on my drawings. I try so hard to make every line perfect. I become frustrated with my inability to capture the precise details of the daffodil—until I realize the irony of it, that I chose a poem called "Failure" and was forcing myself to perfect the poem's illustration. I laid down my pencil and let it be.

I think this is what I need to do more, to let it be—my writing, my drawings, the way I am seen by others, my schoolwork, everything. I worry about all of those things, but I have to realize the beauty in imperfection. As the author writes, even the sky isn't perfect "I know it's marred-/Just another blemish on the earth-" but it is still so beautiful, so pure and the one thing of which we know no end.

Maybe failure is just something we, as humans, have created. Maybe everything is a failure of something else—an A failure to get a B, a short note a failure of a long one, a correct step in a methodical dance just a failure to discover a new way to move.

If this is true, then there is no such thing as failure, is there? There is only what we want and what we earn, or what we decide for ourselves we would like to accomplish. I should not look for redemption by begging forgiveness from the world which never noticed my flaws, but forgive myself, for I have judged myself more than any other. I will join failure for this walk, to see the imperfect sky, "and hand-in-hand, in failure, find redemption."

"Honesty" by Katya E.

I flow in intermittent dazes
(dreaming)
Stumble into reality
(waking)
And drift back out again
Never knowing exactly
Where I've been.
I know what anyone else could tell me, that
I'm suffering from Identity versus Role confusion
(allegedly)
And that Erikson claims this is an adolescent
Standard.
But when I glance at the mirror
To see my lips stained with
Grape popsicle residue,
I do wonder where I belong,
In childhood or this cutthroat real world
Where laugher is just another
Consumer of time.
Sometimes I sink to my bedroom floor
(breathe)
And rest my head on the rough,
Worn, gray carpet, where life
Stretches out infinitely from
My eyes.
Sometimes I just wait there
(aging)
For someone to pick me up, carry me off
But my only companion is Thought
And she is far too unreliable.
I've been told that I am just-
Just one—face in billions
I know that death is inevitable
But life, when realized
Is inevitable too.

(Continues)

(Continued)

I know that you are noticed
When you turn the tides
And send the ocean into raging froth
Foaming in its fury against itself
(revolt)
That it is not considered "important"
To speak to a ripple on the surface
(inconsequential)
Or to show it the surrealist self-portrait
You have painted in a poem.
Who am I to judge whether I should cry out
For one more revolution
Or touch this single wave with my song
But I ask, still—
What matters more, the life or the living?
(revelation)

Madi M.

RESPONSE TO POETS: Naomi Shihab Nye, Mary Oliver, and W. S. Merwin

THOUGHTS ON POETRY

POETRY: "Empty" and "Taking Action" by Madi M.

When I hear the word "poetry," the word itself doesn't come to mind. Instead, I think of color. The deepest purples and brightest yellows, royal blues, and lush greens. A carnival of light and sound explodes in my head. I think of all the poems I've read, all the songs I've heard, all the art work I've seen. Poetry to me is so much more than just a category of writing; it's an art form.

Poetry is different from any other kind of writing. It's musical, personal, unique and beautiful. Poetry can be enjoyed as so much more than just writing on a page. It is not only seen, but heard, felt, tasted, smelt, and appreciated in every sense. So meaningful and so loved.

I like reading Edgar Allen Poe for his complex and mysterious ways. I enjoy the simplicity and plain humor offered by Shel Silverstein. Robert Frost has nice work as well; it's pleasant to read and wonderful to listen to.

Since doing the Heart Book I've really learned to enjoy Naomi Shihab Nye, Anne Turner, and Mary Oliver, as well.

When I look carefully at Madi's responses to poems, I realize each response is a draft of writing that can stand on its own. Poetry touches her, deeply and personally, and leads to crafting more polished poetry of her own.

"How to Paint a Donkey"
by Naomi Shihab Nye

From The Quickwrite Handbook (Rief 2018)

RESPONSE: The piece was a gift for my mother. It was a lopsided pottery piece. I recall that its purpose was to house a candle, of which my mom had countless. I was so proud of my "bee hive," as it was labeled. It was my first present that I myself had gotten/made for my mom. I knew that she would love it, mostly because my five-year-old hands had rendered it imperfect. She would understand and love every crack in the clay, every bump and clump of glaze that would be on the end product. She would cherish my "bee hive" forever; this would be her favorite present from me.

But the beehive never made it to my mom. In fact, the original piece didn't even get into the kiln. My art teacher took one look at my kindergarten creation and ripped off the top half. She told me it was too large. I had to do it again, smaller this time.

Shocked, I started again, angry that the teacher had destroyed my masterpiece. I finished my altered version of the candle holder and allowed her to fire it for me. My mom still has the piece of pottery, but somehow it is not the same. Almost ten years later and what I remember about that candle holder is that what my mom and I would have thought was perfect, was not seen as good enough by my teacher.

"Valentine for Ernest Mann"
by Naomi Shihab Nye

From Red Suitcase (Nye 1994)

RESPONSE: Poetry hides behind my bed, curled up with my sleeping cat. It lives in the nooks and crannies of my very existence, waiting to be found and brought into the light. Poetry hides far up in the tree branches. On the tips of the buds that bloom there. It sneaks into my mind, floating on the sound of waves crashing against the rocky shore. Poetry folds itself into my drawer, neatly tucked away beside my favorite blouse. It is etched in my old rocking chair that creaks as it rocks back and forth. Poetry lingers in the air I breathe; it finds its way into my dreams. Poetry shines through the clouds, illuminating everything with potential. It takes cover behind my curtains. It pours down on me disguised as rain.

"The Journey" by Mary Oliver

From New and Selected Poems (Oliver 1992)

RESPONSE: And then, at that moment, final realization hit. All the time spent trying to please others, all the time wasted trying so desperately to be something other than myself. Finally, it came with perfect clarity. I could be only myself. If I really wanted to be able to live a life worth living, being me would be the answer.

It took me a while to come to this point, and I still often go back to trying to please others and be perfect. But perfection is irrational, and also, undesirable. For who wants to be perfect when there is individuality? I look around to those I love, and to those I aspire to be like. What I notice and cherish most about them are the ways they are unique. I do not pay mind to the mistakes they make and the problems they have, for it would be much stranger if there were an absence of these things. I love their differences, it is what makes them who they are. Doesn't it make sense that I would want them to appreciate those qualities of mine that make me who I am? Me. Once stripped of my behaviors and personality, I am no longer me. Blending in with the "norm" means disappearing altogether. Perfection is not ideal at all; imperfection is what we should strive for.

"Trees" by W. S. Merwin

From The Compass Flower: Poems (Merwin 1977)

RESPONSE: I think of the trees, perhaps the only thing, or certainly one of the few things, that tie us down to the earth. Even as we cut them down, the ones that remain do not falter. They shed silent tears for their destroyed brothers and sister's, and keep on standing tall. Maybe they still have faith in us, maybe they really do think we can turn ourselves around and fix the mess we've made of this beautiful planet. Maybe they know something that we don't, and they'll prove just as wise as I believe them to be. The trees that held me in their branches, the trees that filled my childhood with places to go, places to be alone. Those trees that understand me and listen with such silent love. . . . Trees, the holders of my secrets, the comforters that surround me. So strong. So reliable.

Trees. Standing tall. So strong, like I wish I could be. Graceful, beautiful. . . . Stable, lasting trees.

If only I knew how to grow. Then the scariness and strangeness of getting older would not be so unfamiliar. If only I knew how to grow, then maybe I would not be so afraid of making mistakes. Maybe I could grow gracefully and beautifully, surprising everyone, like the transformation of a caterpillar into a butterfly. What if I could grow like a tree, with determination and purpose? I would grow like I knew what was coming, and never doubt myself. If I knew how to grow I would be surprised by nothing.

But then again, why would I want to know everything about myself? It is much better to discover who you are rather than be sure right from the start? And besides, if I do not know, I have opportunities to create myself along the journey.

So yet again, I have changed my mind. I want to grow clumsily, with the ability to make mistakes and the ability to love the experience of learning. I want to be inexperienced and unsure, going through life like a newborn child and stumbling often. I want my life to be interrupted by new things, different things. Life is a mystery, and I love it.

There is so much to savor in Madi's writing. She thinks and feels deeply, about the universe, about herself, and about her place in this world. **Who am I?** *and* **How do I want to be?** *she asks with her words.*

In her thinking about "Trees" by W. S. Merwin, I wish I had mentioned the writing about trees of William Blake, Hermann Hesse, and Walt Whitman. They had such reverence for the oldest living things on earth.

If the following two picture books had been published while I had Madi in class, I would have recommended them to her:

- ◆ **Wangari Maathai: The Woman Who Planted Millions of Trees** *by Franck Prevot (2015)*

- ◆ **Strange Trees and the Stories Behind Them** *by Bernadette Pourquié and Cécile Gambini (2016)*

"Empty" by Madi M.

A shell remains of what was before;
of what was there exists no more.

The eyes are dull, no light shines through,
her laughs are numbered, her smiles few.

The girl no longer cries because,
she can't recall just who she was.

Unable now to get things right,
she lies awake in bed at night.

Trying again to find her way,
keeping emotions once more at bay.

She reaches out and calls for aid,
as the girl she was appears to fade.

Can they help her, will they know the cure?
Can they stop her bleeding, her internal war?

With love and hope they try their best;
there is only one thing now, the final test.

Can she pull through? Will the fear be gone?
Or will the girl disappear, and the shell live on?

"Taking Action" by Madi M.

There is a sense of change blown in with the warm spring breeze. My ways are to be altered, my health and happiness restored. I am uncovering the true reasons for this problem and taking steps to change behaviors.

I choose to be true to myself and those around me, and to not limit myself with trivial complications. I choose to be part of this world, to hold nothing back and to go forth with purpose and determination.

I will not sit back and allow myself to be created into an unhappy creature. I vow to be my best. I want to give and enjoy. I wish not to harm or to be harmed but to love and receive it. I promise not to give up. I promise to persevere and pull through. I will live.

Arthur T.

PERSUASIVE ESSAY: **"Chess Should Be Included in the K–12 Curriculum" by Arthur T.**

Although Arthur did craft a Heart Book, the cover of which was his Heart Map, he found that the map provided him with as many opportunities to find ideas for his own writing—in the way that Georgia Heard first designed and intended the Heart Maps—as it did for finding poetry and poets that connected to those matters important to him.

He spent a great deal of time in his writer's-reader's notebook talking about chess, eventually turning a lot of his thinking into his persuasive piece, "Chess Should Be Included in the K–12 Curriculum." He also raised money to buy a copy of the documentary film Brooklyn Castle (2012) by director Katie Dellamaggiore to give to our middle school library so all teachers had the opportunity to show it to all students.

As a teacher I had to remind myself that Arthur's obsession with chess was a passion that drove his learning. I tried hard never to crush his enthusiasm by requiring him to write or read about other topics. He could adeptly weave chess into any genre.

Arthur T. Heart Map

Chess Should Be Included
in the K–12 Curriculum

It was Nov 24, 2012 at an event called Burlington Open. I had the white pieces against the top seed, Tian Rossi. The opening in the game was of no interest since it was just two moves into the game. My opponent decided to go into an early endgame. He led an exchange of Rooks. He moved his Rook to e3 challenging my Rook of f3. I took the rook on e3 and he took back with a pawn and then it was my turn. I pictured the board and came up with one move which was the pawn move. I had looked two moves ahead, three moves, four moves, which was to bring my King into the game to decide the game in my favor. Then I saw one move. The only one . . .

* * * * *

Chess should be a subject in the K–12 education, just like math, language arts, social studies, science, world language, and gym. Why chess? Chess, more than any other subject in school, equips you with important life skills, such as accurate decision-making, awareness, observation, calculation, imagination, and active attitudes and actions. When you learn chess, you practice all these life skills.

The objective in chess is to checkmate the opponent's King with pawns and pieces (Queen, Rooks, Bishops, and Knights). To reach the objective, your pieces must be developed so they can work together. Before every move, you must visualize the consequences of the move you are making and take into account that your opponent will be countering your plans.

Chess is art and science combined. Art in chess is creativity—to create new ideas, and to take risks and seize opportunities to achieve goals on the chessboard. Science in chess is seen in that each chess move always has logic behind it. Observation is needed in chess so you can observe your opponent's forces and your own forces, and make the best evaluations and decisions. Observation is one of the requirements to become a great scientist as well as a great chess player.

Chess is a language, not just a fun game. Like the language of English, we use it to communicate, make friends, and express our creativity. In chess, you communicate with different minds at deep levels. Through every chess move, you make a contest dialogue with your opponent. You express your creativity on the chessboard using tactics and imaginations to make brilliant combinations.

Friendship can be created through chess. When someone outplays you, you appreciate the person's talent and the strength of his mind. You meet friends at the chess boards, through game analysis, and you share with them the love for chess.

Strategy in chess helps us in real life. As Emerson put it "The man who knows how, will always have a job. The man who also knows why, will always be his boss." For every chess move, you want to question yourself, "Why this move?" so you can see the cause and effect behind the move. In chess, strategy is the vision and plan to achieve an objective faster than your opponent, taking into account his possibilities, and to prevent your opponent from reaching his objective. In real life, strategy is used to reach objectives in the most efficient ways. Once you learn how to create strategies for your chess games, you can apply that skill anywhere at any time.

Chess helps math because chess requires calculation and mental pictures. Math helps chess also by using calculation. The ability in seeing patterns and analyzing chess positions helps to speed up your mental math. Accuracy is the most important element for chess and math. Math requires problem-solving, which also helps chess because chess also needs problem-solving for unfamiliar and familiar territories on the chessboard. When you have reached a critical moment on the chessboard and in math, critical thinking is required to help solve the problem.

All these elements, strategy, tactics, creativity, focus, and calculations, when integrated together, can bring very positive surprises. Here is an example. In the 2012 National Championship Tournament for K–8 state champions, I defeated the top seed, a chess master. How did a kid from NH who was ranked 23rd out of the 47 players make the big surprise?

I started the game with a strong determination to create active play. After a tense fight in the opening, I decided to offer a pawn for attacking chances, and my opponent fell for my strategy. He took my pawn, thinking that I had made a mistake. As the tense fight continued on, I pushed my mental image deeper and deeper, and saw a tactic to sacrifice my Knight for further attacks. My opponent was tied up to defend. I brought my other Rook into action. All of my power concentrated on my opponent's King as my pieces moved nearer and nearer to his King, attacking mercilessly. My opponent looked at me deeply when we shook hands to end the game. We became friends in that tournament.

I also think that chess should be taught to students who are home-schooled. For example, the Polgar sisters (the top female chess players in the world) were home schooled and their curriculum focused on chess. The Polgar's father taught them chess and the meaning of chess as a whole. The Polgar sisters benefitted from learning chess because their brains sharpened in calculation and analysis. They were creative and imaginative and they were able to have mental pictures in their minds for both math and chess.

Many countries have chess in their school curriculum. For example, Argentina,

Armenia, Great Britain, Venezuela, Hungary, Germany, Spain, Italy, Canada, China, Mexico, Moldova, Peru, USA, and Turkey have schools where chess is a subject being taught. According to research, the students who studied chess had higher grades in math and in English. These students learned through playing chess to visualize the cause and effect of their moves, to plan ahead, and to evaluate before making decisions to move. Patience is required in chess and helps your strategic thinking. Chess in general helps to increase our attention span, so we can learn to be alert and pay attention in any situation. All school districts should include chess in the K–12 education.

• • • • •

Then I saw one move, the only one . . . a simple pawn move to e4 canceling out my opponent's knight and bishop move options. I won the game, after a few more moves, and after a winning endgame for me. Why? My knight was ten times better placed on the board than my opponent's knight, which could only go to four unfortunate directions on the chessboard because my knight was on a central square e4 and had more move options on the chessboard.

One move, the only one . . .

Owen T.

PERSONAL ESSAY: "Off the Dock" by Owen

Owen used his Heart Map to find poetry that mattered to him, but, like many of his classmates, he also used the Heart Map to help find ideas for writing. In a number of cases, the Heart Map and perhaps the reading of the poem by Frederick Morgan, which he found and commented on, often led to some of Owen's finest writing.

Offering students a variety of opportunities for finding writing—Heart Maps, life-maps, a writer's-reader's notebook, quickwrites, photographs, art, op-ed pieces, fiction and nonfiction, just to name a few possibilities—stimulates and supports them with ideas.

Owen T. Heart Map

"I Remember the Sea When I Was Six"
by Frederick Morgan

From Art and Nature *(Farrell 1995)*

RESPONSE: I chose this poem because it is very relatable. As you grow older, you remember and treasure these small, simple moments from when you were little. Being at the beach, tide-pooling, making sand castles, catching anything you could find, toes in the hot sand. They seem like small memories—the smells, the sights, the feelings—but they end up being some of your most treasured moments.

Several weeks after reading "I Remember the Sea . . . ," Owen wrote this personal essay:

"Off the Dock"

The murky shore glistens in the mid-day sun, while water-bugs scamper about the surface, invincible to the water. A garter snake suns himself on the rocks around the fire pit, aware, but unwilling to leave. A beaver swims quietly toward the dam with sticks, and then with a ferocious whack of his tail against the water, plunges under the surface.

The splintered dock underneath me moves only when I do, and the old boat tied up sits anxiously waiting to be used. The worms that were dug up earlier in the garden, wriggle around under leaves and dirt, in a green pail that sits beside me. The cork-handled, but otherwise blue pole, waits for its cue, flip of the bale, and setting of the hook. I sit on the dock, toes dangling in the water; the occasional daring sunfish swims up to see how they taste. The only thing that disturbs the peace on this day is the occasional trolling boat or sound of a car through the woods.

The dog lies on the grass, watching me fish, only halting to raise his head and bark at a passing boat or a small critter. Mosquitoes fly around my head with that dreaded, eerie buzzing sound they make that makes me swat the air. Bees mind their own business, generally, so I don't have too much of a problem with them. Although, I don't want to get too close to a painful sting. Dragonflies and butterflies dance gracefully above the water and land on a nearby bush. Curious turtles pop their heads up through the lily pads, as if from a whack-a-mole machine, then swim undetected to a sunny log, while bullfrogs croak on the shore. Fish jump in the cove, giving away their location with a tail-whip ripple on the surface.

Everything is bright, giving an elated feel to the day, elated and calm. A tug on the end of my line, and I suddenly snap back to reality. So much to see, if you really look around.

Students' Thinking as We Crafted Heart Books

What Students Noticed About Poetry

After producing at least two double-page spreads, which means reading quite a few poems, I ask the students to jot down in their writer's-reader's notebooks what they notice so far about poetry. They then share this information at tables (usually three or four students per table) and reach some consensus about the importance of what they notice about poetry. As a whole class we share a couple of things, write them on the giant sticky note that is posted on the wall, and add to this every month or two with other things "Noticed About Poetry."

It's a good idea to keep lists like this visible to kids. As I talk with them about their writing in any genre, I can point out to them things from this chart. It might be something they did well that other poets do, or asking a question, or giving a suggestion that helps them realize what might be added or done in a way that strengthens the writing.

Added to the list as the year progressed:

- concrete words (*sight, sound, smell, touch, taste*) rather than abstract words (*love, hate, anger, beauty, sadness*) (This is the *show* of "show, don't tell.")
- vivid imagery/paints a picture
- surprising, fresh wording—no clichés or overworked phrases
- selects first and last words/lines carefully—hook that keeps us reading
- sometimes uses repetition for emphasis
- instill any emotion, even fear and terror (e.g., "Wolf Knife" by Donald Hall [1990])
- some make you feel weightless (e.g., "Catch" by Abigail Becker [1993])
- some rhyme, many have no rhyme
- ending might be ambiguous, a question, a message, a shock
- leaves us thinking or feeling something.

This is not meant to be a comprehensive list. It changes every year and only reflects what the kids notice so far in the reading of poetry *this year*. My hope is, as they write their own poetry, they will notice and think about what their writing does.

Noticed about POETRY
- make you think or feel something
- a collection of smaller metaphors that act as a metaphor for a bigger issue
- have a simple but powerful hidden meaning with clues + hints
- puzzle or layers that need to be put together
- nothing is 'scrambled'- every word ties (counts) to topic
- uses similes, metaphors, personification, description (stronger)
- often have to infer happening + meaning
- all have certain rhythm, even without rhyme
- a pattern that differs in each poem
- when read aloud, sounds smooth
- best poems= a dissonance, leave the reader with odd feeling that something is off, and they appreciate it all the more

What students noticed about poetry

What Poets Say About Poetry

As part of their double-page spread, I ask students to find at least three things the poet they chose has to say about poetry or writing or reading. I don't want them doing a bio on the poet, where they list birth, death, books, awards, and so on, unless they find something unusual about the poet, because it really intrigues them. For example, Jimmy Baca began writing poetry in prison.

At the same time that we list what we notice about poetry, I ask the kids to share the words that held significance for them from the poem they chose. "What does your poet say about writing, or reading, or poetry that resonated with you, struck a chord with you?" We add those words to another giant sticky note that we leave on the wall, and add to, throughout the year. As we add to this list, I usually ask the kids, "What do you think Frost meant when he said 'Writing free verse is like playing tennis with the net down'?" (Frost 1935) My hope is that they will find something the poet has to say that makes them think about their own reading and writing, whether they agree or disagree.

Even if you do not have a collection of poetry books in your classroom, kids can find poets' words on numerous sites on the web:

- poetry.org
- press.umich.edu>browse>series
- poetryfoundation.org
- brainyquote.com

Or search by the name of the poet and look for their website, or find poetry sites that list them.

Poets on POETRY

"Poetry: three mismatched shoes at the entrance of a dark alley." Charles Sim

"Poetry is an echo, asking a shadow to dance." Carl Sandburg

"Writing free verse is like playing tennis with the net down." Robert Frost

"The poem is the device through which the ordinary world is seen in a new way engaging, compelling, even beautiful." Ted Kooser

"No tears in the writer, no tears in the reader. No surprise in the writer, no surprise in the reader." Robert Frost

"Instructions for living a life: pay attention, be astonished, tell about it." Mary Oliver

"Writing a poem is like giving blood. It goes straight from the heart of the writer to the heart of the reader." Ralph Fletcher

"Poetry is an orphan of silence. The words never quite equal the experience behind them." Charles S

"A poet is, before anything else, a person who is passionately in love with language." W. H. Auden

What Students Learned About Poetry

I was most interested in hearing what the students had learned for themselves about poetry. What had they noticed as they read poem after poem and collected those poems that meant the most to them? I was astonished at what they learned:

I've noticed that most poems have hidden messages that the author is trying to get you to understand. Trying to figure out what the message or meaning is, is like uncovering a mystery. Some authors hide the meaning or message really well, often in metaphors, while others completely give it away. I also noticed that the way the poet shapes the stanzas really affects the poem.

—Kristen

A lot of poets like to use metaphors . . . sometimes it's more interesting to explain something using a metaphor or personification, like what Carl Sandburg does in "Under a Telephone Pole" [Bolin 1995]: "I am a copper wire slung in the air."

—Caleb

Poetry makes me think, makes me visualize, and brings back memories.

—Kitiara

If you like one poem from a poet, there is a good chance you will like all of their work.

—Morgan

Finding poems you love is like buying shoes; someone else can't do it for you.

—Lindsey

Poetry can sometimes be short and concise, like "Dust of Snow" [Frost 1969] or it can be funny, like "Boy and Mom at the Nutcracker Ballet" [Nye 1998]. [No matter what they write or how they write], poets are passionate about what they write about.

—Brady

I find that poetry often addresses large, broad topics of life. Such as, in "Listen" [Simic 2008] where two people who work in a factory learn what their bombs do. This poem addresses the topic of ignored consequences. "Nothing Gold Can Stay" (Frost in Hinton 1967) addresses how nothing great in life will last forever.

—Thomas

I used to think of rhyming when I thought of poetry, but I haven't found too many poems that rhyme.

—Declan

Poetry seems to be significantly more emotional than prose, and better at carrying feelings, like relaxation or anger or sadness. Even fear can be conveyed in poetry by making the lines short and choppy.

—Henry

If a poem uses punctuation it is very intentional and a lot of thought is put into where it is used. The punctuation determines whether the line is a final statement or open-ended, or waiting for more.

—Lizzy

A lot of poets use repetition. It gives the idea of a loop, and it keeps coming back to one thing and then the poet can break the loop and surprise the reader, invoking powerful emotions. I've never tried repetition in a poem, but seeing it has made me tempted to try it.

—Dylan

There's a lot more to poetry than just words. There are lessons and feelings. Feelings are crucial to make the poem worth reading.

—Rachel

I've noticed that a lot of poems focus on small, simple things but are about much bigger topics. Also, the way that it is written really affects the poem in its entirety; where the spaces between words are, is where the true magic happens. Some poets point out the amazing parts of our world, others pour out their feelings of sadness and anger. No matter the topic/emotion, they always show it through their writing in beautiful and interesting ways.

—Natalie

Poetry is filled with so much more emotion than prose writing usually is. While prose centers around the story of something, poetry focuses on the emotions in that moment.

—Sadie

Poetry is different from other kinds of writing because it has more power in its words. It conveys a message more clearly sometimes than other kinds of writing because it uses the strongest words. Even though many poems have shrouds of mystery in them from metaphors, they still have a way of penetrating deeper into a reader's heart.

—Megan

You need to dig deeper into the poem to find the true meaning. You can't just skim it, and understand it fully. You need to do some thinking.

—Maggie

There are rules even with the rule-less poems.
—Claire

Poetry tends to touch on very deep philosophical subjects, like life, death, love and the passage of time. I think that poets never understand these concepts so they express them in writing.

—Matthew

Poets are trying to get a point down, and they don't want to give you their point, they want you to make your own.

—Madelyn

I always thought poetry had to be short and simple. But reading the poem "If You Forget Me" by Pablo Neruda [Neruda allpoetry .com] made me think otherwise. Not all poems have to be short and to the point to have meaning. . . . Sometimes the message isn't always directly said. Sometimes you have to search for it.

—Kenzie

Poetry is more than just writing, it's like a snapshot of somebody's life . . . it is calming . . . poets write it so they can look back and read it and remember that part of their life.

—Matteo

What I've noticed is that poetry seems ageless, no matter when it was written. When I was looking up quotes from William Blake I was surprised to see he was born so long ago. I didn't expect that because his writing seems so modern. As I looked at the writing of poets now and some, like Blake, from one hundred years ago, there is so much similarity to them in the deeper meanings and how they hid them behind many bright and shiny walls. . . . Poems seem to be crafted to trigger emotions in the

reader. What a reader thinks about in a poem may be different from what other readers think. Poetry seems to be defined by what the reader makes of it.

When I read a poem and gave my meaning to it last year, I wasn't too happy when my teacher told me my answer was wrong. How can you say poetry has one meaning and all others are wrong? Poetry is meant for you to take your meaning from it.

—Amy

Evaluation

Evaluation Form (SEE APPENDIX, P. 187)

*I*t's a sad fact that for many of the students who ask, "Does this count?" they mean, "Are you grading these?" It's another sad fact that when I did not grade these, some students did not put in their best effort. The more the students became involved in finding poems that spoke to them and spent time planning, playing with, and crafting their illustrations, the less the evaluation form mattered to them.

EVALUATION FORM

I settled on the evaluation form I included in the Appendix of this book (see page 187), which I tuck inside each Heart Book. Every four to six weeks I expect to see a double-page spread, read it, and evaluate each section with + (item was there) or ++ (item done exceptionally, thoughtfully, and thoroughly). And yes, the + translates into a **B**, and the ++ an **A**. If an item is missing or done with insufficient information, students have the option to redo it or complete it. I admit that parts of this evaluation are subjective, especially their responses to the poem and their illustrations. I admit that the student's effort plays a large part in my assessment.

My goals are to help students get to know poets, to find poetry that means something to them. Poems that stretch their thinking and beliefs about themselves and the world. If the reading and crafting of these Heart Books help them discover that poetry is not *dumb and stupid and a waste of time*, as many students have believed, I am satisfied. If they show what Tom Romano often calls *good faith participation* in these Heart Books I am satisfied with all they have done.

TALKING WITH STUDENTS AS THEY WORK

Just as I would while students are working on any writing, I am moving around, table by table, student by student. Just as I would in any writing I am sticking with a format that seems to help them as much as it helps me as a writer:

Liked/Noticed/Heard/Stayed with me

Question/s

Suggestion/s: What if. . .

I am first pointing out what strikes me about their work and/or what they are doing well. Then I might ask a question or two, and/or make a suggestion. In the case of the Heart Books, it might look like this:

That watercolor wash bleeds beautifully into the Oliver poem.

Love the way you laid out the Simic quotes on your two pages.

That is some sophisticated thinking about Stafford's choice of words.

You really made a personal connection with that poet. Loved the way you said. . .

What words or images made you feel sad (or angry or happy) as you read his poem?

In what ways did the poet's decision not to use any punctuation affect the way you read the poem? Or understood it?

What attracted you to this poem?

In what ways are your experiences with *basketball* (with *siblings*, with. . .) similar or different from the poet's?

The poet uses present tense throughout the poem—what does that do to you as a reader?

I know you love football and basketball. What if you look at *American Sports Poems*?—It has an index by subject in the back of the book. I bet you could find a poem you will like.

I think you'd love Kwame Alexander or Nikki Giovanni. What if you try one of those poets next time?

What if you use watercolor paper instead of painting directly on the pages in the blank book? See if that keeps the paint from bleeding or soaking through.

I'd love to be able to read the poem and your thinking, but a #3 pencil is nearly impossible for me to read. Here's a fine point pen with black ink you might try.

Just as I would in any class where the students are engaged in their work, and I don't want to interrupt them, I put my name on the board with the note:

If I can help you in any way, write your name on the board.

Then I am moving table by table, student by student. Stopping when it seems appropriate to notice with a compliment, or question, or suggestion.

If students choose to, they have every opportunity to redo an item or redo the entire double-page spread before finding the next poem. Or they can learn from that one page what to put more effort into the next time. At the end of the year, students can choose the three double-page spreads they are most proud of for their final Heart Book averaged evaluation.

Art Walk: Students Reading and Commenting on Peers' Heart Books

At the end of the year we have an art walk, where students leave their Heart Book on the table at the place where they sit, with three-to-five blank sticky notes near the book. Every student has to move around the room, reading at least one Heart Book at each table and leaving a sticky note commenting on what they notice/learn/enjoy most from one spread or about the entire Heart Book. Each note has to be signed by the reader. If we had more time (always the

Art walk: students writing comments to each other

dilemma), I would have done this more often, at least at the end of each quarter so kids could get more ideas from each other. An audience lifts the students' efforts, if they know peers or others will be looking at their work.

Another possibility is setting each Heart Book on an art stand in the library for several weeks for the entire school to enjoy. I like the blank books from Bare Books because they include a plastic cover for each book for a few more cents, and this protects the book that is handled throughout the entire year.

This is the kind of assessment that I value the most: students' reflections. In an earlier section of this book I shared students' thinking about poetry before we did the Heart Books. The changes since doing the Heart Books are significant. In anything we do with students, their reflections before and after a project or study help us plan, revise, rethink, and frankly, even abandon, our ideas, based on their feedback.

Students' Thoughts on Poetry After the Heart Books

Please note that other students' thinking is also on the pages taken directly from their Heart Books as seen in the section "Students' Reconstructed Heart Book Pages." The students cited here do not have their Heart Book pages in this book, but what they learned from doing them is meaningful information to gather about the validity of doing such a project. There are so many others I wish I could have included.

In Section Seven I summarize what I learned from reading the students' reflections that changes their minds about poetry. What lingers in my head and my heart are the words of these young men and women, like Domi: "Poetry is what whispers in the wind, only to the people that want to hear it. Poetry is like music, it floats and lingers in the air. Poetry lives in waterfalls, falling beautiful and cleansing. It lives within all of u, we just have to find it."

STUDENTS' THOUGHTS ON POETRY AFTER THE HEART BOOKS

Before I did these Heart Books I thought poetry was one big, fat eyeroll. I thought it was boring and annoying and pointless. I thought it was corny and too lovey-dovey. Last year in our poetry unit, the poems our teacher picked weren't poems that I was interested in. They were boring. Now that we get to pick the ones we want to put in our book they are actually about stuff I have done and like. They are actually interesting. I can relate more to the poet and understand why he put those words together.

Since doing the Heart Book I noticed that it is a true art to get the perfect words to match up and be perfect yet simple. I also noticed that less is more. Everybody I know likes shorter poems. Most adults think that's just because they are lazy, but really people think it's cool when someone can put so much depth into something with 20 words. I can't even send a text without doing that. —*Haley*

Before the Heart Book the only poets I was familiar with were Emily Dickinson, Robert Frost, and Shakespeare. I didn't know that poems could be as short as four lines, or one stanza. I thought that poetry was less-used language, like old English. I didn't realize that I hear poetry every day, in the music I listen to. I thought that poetry was ancient, something from the past that did not concern me, and really wouldn't come up in my life unless I reached for it.

However, in making the Heart Book, I realized that poetry is a free way of writing. You follow a beat, such as in music, and sometimes it's a beat that only you can hear. But when others hear it too, that's when your writing becomes famous. . . . If writing comes from the heart, it is true beauty. —*Siobhan*

Even before we did the Heart Books, I knew that poetry was a more free and expressive form of writing. In other grades I read poetry anthologies, read novels written in verse, and had written some of my own pieces. I learned about different types of poetry: free verse, couplets, limericks, acrostic poems, etc. I knew that many of my classmates did not like poetry because it was "boring" or "stupid." However, I disagreed. I *love* poetry. Whether I was reading or writing it, I was always enjoying myself. Just the fluidity that a poem possesses mesmerized me, and I loved working on a piece to make it as fluid as the poems I read by famous authors. I think the reason I loved it so much is because I could relate to it. My two hobbies were, and are, figure-skating and dance. The main reason why these art forms and sports are so compatible is the artistry and *fluidity*; also, these are activities that require strength, which many people overlook. Poems are the same, with not only an artistic and fluid side, but each poem contains a certain strength that can be seen by the "trained eye." —*Kailey*

Before the heart book, I only knew what I learned from prior years of poetry units. How to craft a poem and the different styles of poetry, but *never* have I had an assignment that included my opinion on the poetry, or how I could relate to it. Before this, I honestly just didn't like poetry. Simple as that. I had always enjoyed writing it, but when I read others' poetry, I could never understand the true meanings. It could be because in prior years we never got choices on what type of poetry we would like to read. We read what the teachers would assign us to read, and that was that. I guess I just thought we'd never get much choice . . . that's why I didn't like it. Read it—say what it's about. Never to say how it might relate to you.

Since doing the Heart Book I've noticed that poetry is very similar to music, one of my favorite things in the world. My favorite songs are based on how much I can relate to them. I've noticed that my favorite poems are based on how I can relate to them. —*Sedona*

Before we started the Heart Books I was not very familiar with poetry. In elementary school, we read Shel Silverstein. I wasn't a fan of his because most of his poems were about something silly. I didn't know any other poets or poems, so because I didn't like his poems, I didn't like poetry.

In seventh grade we did a unit on poetry. We read lots of poems the teacher chose and wrote our thoughts of them in our journals. Learning poetry by interpreting was hard for me because I have trouble thinking through the poems, and that is all we did. The Heart Books were a more enjoyable way to experience poetry because we could choose poems that were meaningful to us. We could express our feelings for the poem and be creative in the way we illustrated it.

I noticed that many authors write about things they have experienced or are passionate about. An example is "Libraries" by Langston Hughes [Medina 2002]. I learned that poetry is more than just a bunch of rhyming words in a random format. I noticed that not all poetry rhymes, and in fact, the majority of the poetry in the world does not.   —*Erica*

Before doing the Heart Book, the only poetry I read was on tumblr and it's anonymous. I like it because no matter what the topic is, I can always relate to it. Now that I've done the Heart Book I think about the little things in the world and how they shape us: how the grass pricks at my skin when the wind blows, how my eyes squint when the sun hits them, how my eyelashes tickle my eyelids when I look up too far. Little things.   —*Lindsey*

I always thought poetry was boring, confusing, and didn't have a point. I didn't like poetry at all. I thought it was useless. But the Heart Book has made me completely change my mind. I used to read poems and think they made no sense whatsoever, but now I realize they were probably just metaphors for something different. These Heart Books have exposed me to poetry and after I look at each poem I've collected I notice I am loving poetry more and more, especially the ones I can connect with. Each month I enjoyed reading through different poems and finding one that fit. It was almost like trying on clothes, figuring out what size and style fits your body type.   —*Kristen*

Before doing the Heart Book I thought poetry was boring and kind of girly. I thought it was a way for artists to complain, that it was made to draw attention to them. I really didn't get the point of it and just didn't like it. I couldn't understand why people could be so caught up in stupid poetry. . . . I knew poetry was supposed to be beautiful, but I just couldn't see it.

Since we did the Heart Book I noticed that poetry is not just some junk writing that was thrown together by wadded up pieces of paper they found in the garbage, but really can have a lot of meaning and be quite beautiful. I really have noticed the comedy, love, and compassion people put in their poetry to express themselves. I no longer think that whiney people with lives that are great are complaining, writing it down on paper, and calling it poetry. It is really amazing the amount of emotion that they put into the writing. It makes you feel what they feel, or at least be able to relate to it.

Jimmy Santiago Baca surprised me because he was abused as a child and went to jail. To be able to write about that is amazing. Sharing a poem is one thing, but sharing a traumatic story to the whole world is another. To have such a bad childhood and go to jail for five years would crush me. . . . Somehow, he found his way through poetry..   —*Wayne*

(Continues)

Before doing the Heart Book I thought that poetry was awful and useless. I didn't see a point to it. Why should I read poetry when I could just sit down with a good book? Poetry was confusing and made no sense to me. Why wouldn't the author just say what they wanted to say? Why did they have to bother with lines and rhyming? I just didn't understand it.

Since doing the Heart Book, after reading hundreds of poems, and finding many that I like, I've learned that poetry *does* have meaning. It's a way to get a message across that no other writing can. It can convey emotion without words. Just in the way the lines break can show an emotion. Longer fluid lines give a sense of ease and comfort. Choppy, short lines give a more shocked and uneasy mood. Rhymes give poems a nice flow. The white space is just as important as the actual words. It groups things together, giving space for the reader to think.

Naomi Shihab Nye surprised me the most. She puts herself into every one of her poems. She relates all of her poems to herself and her experiences. Through her poems it is clear what is important to her: family and heritage. These are things we can all relate to.   **—Yasmine**

I thought that poetry was the worst thing in the world. I hated it. Every time poetry came up in LA [language arts] class I wanted to scream. I thought this because of 4th grade. We had to write poems about what the teacher wanted you to write. You didn't see any examples. You just had to write. And you had to share your poem no matter how bad it was. I hated it.

Before doing the Heart Books I thought that the only good thing about poetry was that poems were short. Now that we are done, I admit I enjoyed the poems, and though I won't admit it out loud, I think that in high school I'd enjoy taking a course on poetry.   **—Greg**

Before doing these Heart Books I thought very little of poetry. I didn't care about it and didn't want to have anything to do with it. I did one thing with poetry—stereotyped it. I always thought that only girls can write or read poems because I thought poetry was happy and fun, like someone skipping through a flower meadow. I didn't think poetry was good for anything. I thought it was a lazy way of writing. Only people who couldn't use big enough words to describe what they were thinking wrote poetry. I also believed that all poems had to rhyme because the only poets I had read were Dr. Seuss and Shel Silverstein. I don't think these things anymore.

Since doing the Heart Book, what I noticed before about poetry was completely wrong. I noticed that even if I make the slightest bit of effort I will find a piece of poetry that relates to me in some way, which was the biggest reason why I didn't read it because I couldn't find anything that interested me. I also learned that poetry is NOT for just girls. I learned that a lot of famous men have written very good pieces of poetry and made a good living off of this.   **—Casey**

What Changes Kids' Minds About Poetry?

Certain conditions need to be present in the classroom to get our students to rethink their negative perceptions about poetry. We need to make sure the room is filled with the voices of writers like our students, so they can find themselves, yet also make sure it is filled with the voices of those outside the students' experiences, so they can see how the world might be so different from their limited lives. Just as in a writing-reading workshop, students can do their best work when given choices, time, mentor texts, and positive responses that keep them growing stronger both intellectually and emotionally. This is what works best:

- Give kids *choices* into which poems or poets they read.

- Surround students with poems from both contemporary and classic poets from multicultural backgrounds.

- Help students find poems that connect to their very core, those things that matter most to them.

- Help students find poems that allow them to see the world in ways they don't usually see the world.

- Provide time to find those poems, time to read them, time to hear them, and time to reflect on the poem through talking, writing, and drawing.

- Ask open-ended questions about the poetry they read:

  - What came to mind as you read this poem?

  - What did the poem make you think or feel?

  - What in the poem made you think or feel that way?

  - What did you notice about the way the poem was written?

  - What did the poet do that you might try in your own writing?

Elisa New, a professor of American literature at Harvard University and the creator and PBS host of *Poetry in America*, suggests the following about teaching poetry:

- Choose poems that allow students to tap into their own experience, but also stretch beyond that experience.

- Instead of asking, "What does this poem mean?" ask, "What is the first word that slows you down or stops you? Why? Others?"

- Teach formal technical aspects of a poem only when needed, letting students create a glossary of terms they need to express observations. These technical aspects (jargon) can be overwhelming and alienating. Students don't need it.

- Give students a chance to build their own experiences with poetry.

I also want to remember Amy Clark's words:

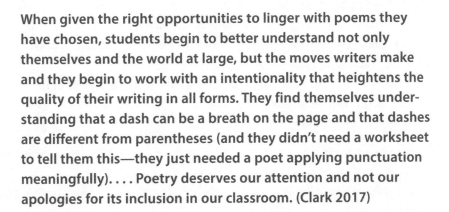

When given the right opportunities to linger with poems they have chosen, students begin to better understand not only themselves and the world at large, but the moves writers make and they begin to work with an intentionality that heightens the quality of their writing in all forms. They find themselves understanding that a dash can be a breath on the page and that dashes are different from parentheses (and they didn't need a worksheet to tell them this—they just needed a poet applying punctuation meaningfully). . . . Poetry deserves our attention and not our apologies for its inclusion in our classroom. (Clark 2017)

Repeat after Amy Clark (and me): "Poetry deserves our attention and not our apologies for its inclusion in our classroom."

AFTERWORD

In the spring of 2020, just as the world was shutting down from the Covid-19 pandemic, and just as I was writing a new proposal with a revised draft of this book, schools began to close and resort to online learning. My writing didn't feel important or urgent. Will poetry matter to teachers and students? Will reading poetry matter to anyone? Doubts crept in.

One publisher, a year earlier, had rejected my proposal with "Poetry books don't sell . . . Art doesn't sell . . ." I heard, in the silences between their words: Creativity is out . . . Standards are in . . . Kids hate poetry . . . Teachers don't know how to teach it.

I was ready to abandon the idea—return all kids' work to folders in file crates. And then I read an article in the *New York Times*, in which Marc Lacey, the assistant managing editor, says:

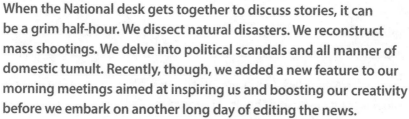

When the National desk gets together to discuss stories, it can be a grim half-hour. We dissect natural disasters. We reconstruct mass shootings. We delve into political scandals and all manner of domestic tumult. Recently, though, we added a new feature to our morning meetings aimed at inspiring us and boosting our creativity before we embark on another long day of editing the news.
We read a poem. (Lacey NYT, March 5, 2020)

I thought, if poetry matters in this way—"the magic of poetry—it jolts your mind into thinking about a subject or theme in an unexpected way"—to the editorial staff at the *New York Times*, surely it has to matter to others. This article, and reading through the students' work I had collected from the Heart Books, reenergized me.

I reread the students' thoughts and beliefs about poetry, their thinking about the poems they found and liked; I looked closely at their responses to poems, resaw the work they put into their illustrations. Everything they noticed about poetry pushed their thinking. Poetry mattered to them. It mattered even before the pandemic struck and changed their lives. If poetry mattered to them, it mattered to me. I went back to reorganizing and rewriting.

In January 2021, as I reviewed, rethought, and continued to revise every page of this book, something happened that told me beyond any doubt that poetry touches our lives in so many ways. Amanda Gorman.

Amanda Gorman. Her name is worthy of repetition. Again and again. Amanda Gorman. America's first Youth Poet Laureate. A twenty-two-year-old Harvard graduate. On January 6, in Washington, DC, at the inauguration of Joe Biden, our forty-sixth president of the United States, Amanda Gorman stepped to the podium and delivered her poem "The Hill We Climb," written specifically for this occasion. With her words and her delivery, she wowed the world and rendered it speechless. The poetry collection she hadn't even finished writing, *The Hill We Climb*, that wouldn't be out until September 2021, shot to the top of the *New York Times* best-seller list on January 7.

Every teacher in the United States, and perhaps even in the world, had their lesson plan for the next day: listen to Amanda Gorman. If you did not do that, you can still do it, now and year after year:

First reading—Watch and listen to Amanda Gorman read her poem "The Hill We Climb" (easily found online).

Second reading—Hand out copies of her poem to each student. Ask them to underline any phrases that resonate (stand out, feel important) to them, or with them, as *you* now read the poem aloud to them. Have students go back to one of the underlined phrases and for two to three minutes write anything that comes to mind, letting the line lead their thinking. If students want to, let them share their writing aloud.

Third reading—Do what Kylene Beers calls a "Pointed Reading" (Beers 1987). Tell your students you are going to read the entire poem to them again, and as you come to lines they underlined they should join you in the reading of those lines aloud. This is a powerful way to read any poem aloud—hearing classmates' voices in lines they feel are important and seeing the differences in those lines that really stood out. You can end with this Pointed Reading or talk through what students noticed about the poetry, about themselves. What did they take to heart from Gorman's words? In what ways did the poem change them?

Yes, poetry matters and deserves its place in our lives, in our work, and in our classrooms. I hope that collecting student thinking, through their reading, writing, and art, helps your students gain insight into all that's important in their lives. I hope poetry offers comfort and, also, some discomfort. Yes, discomfort, in a way that leads all kids to even deeper compassion for others, for all those whose lives and experiences they have not had and can only imagine. For many of them, I hope the reading and writing of poetry, become a "jolt" that makes them see themselves and others in "unexpected ways" (Lacey 2020).

Heart Book Instructions

1. Glue this page onto the first page in your blank book. Turn the page.

2. On the *left side* of the first double-page spread, answer the following questions:

   What comes to mind when you hear the word *poetry*?

   What makes poetry different from other kinds of writing?

   Who are your favorite poets? What do you like about their poetry?

3. Leave the *right side* of this first double-page spread *blank for now*.

   We are going to fill our Heart Books with poetry. Choose your poems because they reflect something from your Heart Map. The poems you choose should reflect you and/or people, places, activities, issues, beliefs, or things that you care about deeply. Every few weeks you will add a poem to this poetry collection. You may *type or handwrite* the poems and your thinking on these pages. Date each poetry entry.

4. On one side of the double-page spread:
   - Write the date.
   - Copy the poem and its author, book, or source used.
   - Illustrate the poem (with paintings, drawings, photos, diagrams, designs, etc.).

5. On the other side of the double-page spread:
   - Explain why you chose this poem, what you notice about it, and how it means something to you.
   - Write down:
     - what the poet has to say about poetry, about writing, about reading (in other words, *quote the poet*)
     - anything of interest about the poet
     - sources used—book, website, other.

I recommend the following poets:

Kwame Alexander	Ralph Fletcher	Ron Koertge	Ntozake Shange
Sherman Alexie	Robert Frost	Ted Kooser	William Shakespeare
Maya Angelou	Nikki Giovanni	George Ella Lyon	Tupac Shakur
Jimmy Santiago Baca	Eloise Greenfield	Eve Merriam	Shel Silverstein
Abigail Becker	Nikki Grimes	Walter Dean Myers	Charles Simic
William Blake	Donald Hall	Pablo Neruda	Clint Smith
Gwendolyn Brooks	Seamus Heaney	Naomi Shihab Nye	Gary Soto
Sandra Cisneros	Georgia Heard	Mary Oliver	William Stafford
Lucille Clifton	Sara Holbrook	Linda Pastan	Walt Whitman
Billy Collins	Langston Hughes	Marge Piercy	Richard Wilbur
E. E. Cummings	Paul Janeczko	Edgar Allan Poe	William Carlos Williams
Emily Dickinson	Rupi Kaur	Jack Prelutsky	Jacqueline Woodson
Tom Feelings	Sarah Kay	Carl Sandburg	

You may choose any poets from the anthologies on my shelves. You might find poems that really speak to you in the novels written in poetry: Jason Reynolds, Kwame Alexander, Meg Kearney, Thanhhà Lại . . .

Try finding a variety of poets, especially ones you have never read before. What poets would you add to this list?

Art Invitations

Why Art in the English/Language Arts Classroom?

In this 20th century, to stop rushing around, to sit quietly on the grass, to switch off the world and come back to the earth, to allow the eye to see a willow, a bush, a cloud, a leaf, . . . I have learned that what I have not drawn I have never really seen.

—FREDERICK FRANCK (1973) *THE ZEN OF SEEING*

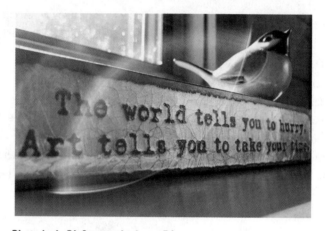

Photo by L. Rief; quote by Junot Díaz

It never fails. After any workshop or presentation I do that embodies art to some degree in my eighth-grade classroom, a teacher asks, "So what do I tell my administrator when she comes by and says, 'Why are you letting middle school students draw?'"

So long as we think any kind of art is frivolous, and only for little kids, I will continue to get such questions.

I want to turn to one book, Peggy Albers' (2007) *Finding the Artist Within*, and the research she cites, particularly from Elliot Eisner and Kay Cowan. From Albers:

In the United States, those making decisions about curriculum value efficiency and content which can be tested scientifically. . . . The arts, because they cannot be encapsulated in a standardized test or measured scientifically, have little room in the curriculum. Eisner's (1982, 1991, 1992, 2002a, 2002b, 2003a, 2003b) research studies in the arts indicate that the arts do not just teach students to feel about the world, or engage in the *affective*, but they also teach students to see, notice, and critically interrogate the world, or engage the *cognitive*.

According to Eisner (1998),

If education as a process is aimed at expanding and deepening the kinds of meanings that people can have in their lives, and if literacy is conceptualized as a process concerned with the construction and communication of meaning, then school programs must attempt to provide time for the development of multiple forms of literacy. (16)

The genuinely good school increases individual differences. . . . A genuine educational process cultivates productive idiosyncrasy, it does not homogenize children into standardized forms. (18)

Literacy is far more than being able to read or to write. . . . When we include forms of representation such as art, music, dance, poetry, and literature in our programs, we not only develop forms of literacy, we also develop particular cognitive potentialities. What one does not or is not permitted to use, one loses. Mind is a form of cultural achievement, and the school programs we develop and implement help define the kinds of minds that children will be given an opportunity to own. (18)

One would think, given the importance of imagination, that it would be regarded as one of the basics of education. (26)

The act of making something is not only an occasion for expressing or representing what you already know, imagine, or feel, it is also a means through which the forms of things unknown can be uncovered. And because what they know cannot always be projected through the logical use of language, they should have a variety of options available and the skills with which to use them. (27)

Albers (2007) reinforces all that Eisner knows and says.

First, the arts require that learners pay attention to the relationships that exist within any text, whether it be a story, poem, artwork, or musical composition.

Second, the arts, by nature, invite problem-solving and
complex thinking. Although schools would argue that they want
learning to be divergent, imaginative, or creative, standardized
testing promotes convergent or single-track thinking (Arts
Education Partnership 2005; Eisner 2002b). Complex thinking
revolves around searching out many possible solutions or
interpretations rather than looking solely for a right answer.

Third, the arts promote paying attention to the way a text is
configured. Focusing on how a story is written, how the words in
a poem are chosen, how an artwork is presented . . . encourages
learners to pay attention not only to what someone is expressing,
but how what is being expressed is constructed. (11)

K. W. Cowan (2001a, 2001b), in her study of the composing processes
of fifth-grade students, concluded that when the arts are a part of literacy
instruction:

1. students write with force and interest;

2. art and language operate as reciprocal processes, both dependent on the
   other for clarity in and extension of meaning making;

3. students learn to pay attention to details in both written and artistic
   texts, and understand how to use language and art to create shades of
   meaning; and

4. students "feel on fire" (Cowan, 2001b, p.122) when the visual arts are
   part of literacy learning. (Albers 2007, 13)

Cowan's students met and exceeded state and national standards in literacy.
In subsequent work, Cowan studied in depth the relationship among the arts,
literacy, and achievement:

> I realized that the visual and performing arts, by their very nature, connect the student to both affect and cognition, and there is an increased energy in the learning experience. The experience takes on an emotive quality and the student easily moves to higher-order thinking processes, and remembers the content long after it has been taught. Beyond this major advantage of an integrated approach . . . assessment ranging from vocabulary development to comprehension of text to writing in a meaningful way cuts across many standards. This often is not the case when skills are taught in isolation. (Cowan and Albers 2006, 134–35)

Smith and Wilhelm (2002), in their seminal study of boys and reading, discovered the following:

> For the boys in our study, the intense importance of the visual as they engaged with all forms of text was evident, and we believe it cannot be oversold. The few engaged readers in this study all described their reading of books and stories in strikingly visual terms. The other boys described their engagement with visual or multimedia texts, such as movies and cartoons, in much the same enthusiastic way as the engaged readers described their reading. . . . All of the boys insisted that the best materials were highly visual or stimulated visual thinking. Engaged readers like Neil said to read well, it had to be a visual experience. It was important to "see" what he was reading. (151–52)

Furthermore, Alexandra Mae Jones, writing for CTV News in Toronto on October 4, 2020, reported that a study out of Norway suggests that handwriting and drawing engage the brain far more than typing on a keyboard, after measuring the brain activity of children and young adults performing these tasks. The research, published this past summer in the journal *Frontiers in Psychology* (2020), looked at a small sample size of twelve children and twelve young adults. The authors had studied the topic before in 2017 by looking at the brain activity of twenty students, but this new study is the first to include children.

Audrey van der Meer, a neuroscientist and professor at the Norwegian University of Science and Technology, said in an October press release that due to an increased reliance on the digital sphere, "we risk having one or more generations lose the ability to write by hand." After analyzing the brain activity taken from the experiment, researchers found that areas of the brain correlated with working memory and encoding new information were more active during handwriting (and drawing).

When Albers says, "Although schools would argue that they want learning to be divergent, imaginative, or creative, standardized testing promotes convergent or single-track thinking," I have to wonder, are these the schools that have Bloom's taxonomy printed in a large poster pinned to the office wall? At the top of that pyramid, designed by Vanderbilt University Center for Teaching, sits the one word, *create*. This framework of educational goals elaborated by Benjamin Bloom and his collaborators in 1956 has been used for generations as a framework for educational goals by K–12 teachers and college instructors. *Create*, at the pinnacle of the framework pyramid, means to "produce new or original work" through design, assembly, construction, conjecture, development, formulation, authoring or investigation. I further have to wonder, do these schools use standardized test scores as their gauge of growth in their students? A sad and inexplicable irony that exists in too many of our schools.

What have I personally noticed in the classroom when I've asked students to visually represent their thinking? It slows them down, inviting them to linger in the words as they read and reread their poems to determine the best way to illustrate all they notice. In their art they play with the relationship between words and images: Which type of art? Vivid or soft colors or black and white? Realistic figures or imagined shapes? Size of images? Facial expressions? Endless decisions they must consider for an illustration. Looking at the various artwork students did, shows us what they noticed about tone, stance, and idea in the poems they chose. Their illustrations demonstrate an analysis of the poem as much as their responses in words do.

If anyone asks, "Why are you encouraging, using, and producing art in the English language arts classroom?" hand them a copy of these pages. In the words of Junot Díaz, "Art tells you to take your time."

References*

*(specifically focused on "Why Art in the English Language Arts Classroom?)

Albers, Peggy. 2007. *Finding the Artist Within*. Newark, DE: International Reading Association.

Armstrong, P. 2010. Bloom's Taxonomy. Vanderbilt University Center for Teaching. https://cft.vanderbilt.edu/guides-sub-pages/blooms-taxonomy/.

Askvik, Eva Ose, F. R. (Ruud) van der Weel, and Audrey L. H. van der Meer. 2020. "The Importance of Cursive Handwriting over Typewriting for Learning in the Classroom" *Frontiers in Psychology.* https://www.frontiersin.org /articles/10.3389/fpsyg.2020.01810/full.

Cowan, K. W. 2001a. "The Arts and Emergent Literacy." *Primary Voices K–6* 9 (4): 11–18.

———. 2001b. *The Visual-Verbal Connections of Literacy: An Examination of the Composing Processes of the Fifth- and Sixth-Grade Student.* Unpublished doctoral dissertation. Georgia State University, Atlanta.

Cowan, K. W., and P. Albers. 2006. "Semiotic Representations: Building Complex Literacy Practices Through the Arts." *The Reading Teacher* 60 (2): 124–37.

Eisner, Elliot W. 1982. *Cognition and Curriculum: A Basis for Deciding What to Teach.* New York: Longman.

———. 1991. "What the Arts Taught Me About Education." In: *Reflections from the Heart of Educational Inquiry: Understanding Curriculum and Teaching Through the Arts*, edited by G. Willis and W. H. Schubert, 34–48. Albany, NY: State University of New York Press.

———. 1992. "The Misunderstood Role of the Arts in Human Development." *Phi Delta Kappan* 73 (8): 591–95.

———. 1998. *The Kind of Schools We Need: Personal Essays.* Portsmouth, NH: Heinemann.

———. 2002a. *The Arts and the Creation of Mind.* New Haven, CT: Yale University Press.

———. 2002b. "What Can Education Learn from the Arts About the Practice of Education?" *Journal of Curriculum and Supervision* 18 (1): 4–16.

———. 2003a. "The Arts and the Creation of Mind." *Language Arts* 80 (5): 340–44.

———. 2003b. "Artistry in Education." *Scandinavian Journal of Educational Research* 47 (3): 373–84.

Franck, Frederick. 1973. *The Zen of Seeing.* Visalia, CA: Vintage Books.

Jones, Alexandra Mae. 2020. "New Study Suggests Handwriting Engages the Brain More Than Typing." (Oct. 4). CTV News. Toronto, CA.

Smith, Michael, and Jeffrey Wilhelm. 2002. *Reading Don't Fix No Chevys.* Portsmouth, NH: Heinemann.

Contour Drawing and Watercolor

The French word *contour* means "outline." Contour drawing forces the artist to pay attention to the general size of an object and its distinct lines.

Because the Art Invitations are not the central focus of this book, I make them as simple as possible. And because I only have the students for 45–50 minutes per day, I try to use the time for double duty: teaching *contour drawing* and *watercolor* techniques at the same time. In addition, not only does the watercolor art the students create teach them the process, in case they want to try this for an illustration in their Heart Book, but it also allows them to use this art on the cover of a card that becomes a gift of writing to a parent or grandparent during the holiday season. (Triple duty!)

Try This: Contour Drawing

Materials

A simple object: a leaf, a shell, the student's own hand

Watercolor paper—preferably 140 bond, cut into 4.25 × 5.5-inch rectangles

(Watercolor paper can be expensive. This is enough to learn the process.)

Sharpie permanent marker—black, ultrafine point

(If you don't use a permanent marker, the ink will bleed into the water when you apply it to the paper.)

Directions

I instruct students: "You're drawing the outside edges but you are not tracing them. Starting at what seems to be a beginning point of an object, follow its outer edges with your eyes, as you glance back and forth at the paper from the object as you draw the contour." (I add a few inner lines to give the object depth, but only the outer lines are contour lines.) I tell the students to fill the paper, big enough to work with watercolor.

In the case of the shell, I leave off any sharp protrusions, as it is harder to put water around small areas compared with wide-open space. With any object you can put paint inside *or* outside the object.

Try This: Watercolor

Materials

Watercolor paint sets (Crayola is fine.)

Variety of brush sizes

Two cups of clear water:

> One for brushing clear water on paper

> One for rinsing brush as colors added

Watercolor paper with contour drawings of any variety of natural objects

(It works best to have one watercolor set, several brushes, and two plastic cups for every two students.)

Directions

Wet on wet wash is the easiest (the watercolor does the work) and most successful method I know for working with watercolor. It lends itself beautifully to creating scenes in nature (sunrise, sunset, the ocean, a river, a meadow, a garden, etc.) or recreating natural objects (leaf, shell, flower, tree, rock, etc.).

Have students write their names on the back of their contour drawings. Using the leaf design, or whatever you choose to use for the contour drawing, have students fill the *inside* of the object with *clear water*. It should be puddle wet with a glossy sheen to it that you can see when you hold the paper up to the light. Once the object is filled with water, start to touch colors to it. The colors will run, and will only go where there is water.

I put the water on the shell design *outside* the shell. Remember, the colors only run where there is water. If there is too much water, a tissue touched

to the spot will absorb the water. If there is not enough water, more clear water can be added. I remind students to never leave brush tips sitting in water. It will ruin the bristles.

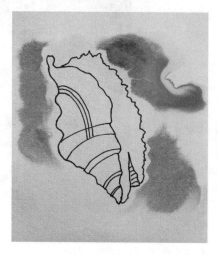 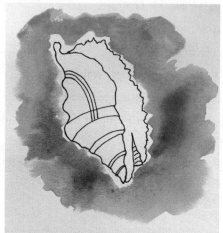

There are numerous good websites online that teach contour drawing and watercolor techniques. All of these are worth watching and trying with your students, if you have the time. I did not try all of these with my students, but I did recommend the following YouTube videos to them in the same way I would recommend a mentor text to them for something they were trying or wanted to know more about.

"Contour Line Drawing Tutorial" posted by user OnlineDrawingLessons on July 11, 2011.

"Watercolor Techniques—Plastic Wrap" posted by user Ms. Covart on March 7, 2017.

"Basic Watercolor Techniques 3—Wet in Wet Washes" posted by user The Mind of Watercolor on October 17, 2014 (Steve Mitchell of MindofWatercolor.com, shows clearly how to put wet on wet, color onto clear water, color onto clear water that has been put over a bone-dry flat wash, or a graduated wash of wet on wet on a bone-dry flat wash.).

"3 Simple Tricks for Unique Watercolor Textures" posted by user Every Tuesday on October 4, 2016 (Teela Cunningham shows the different textures one can achieve with salt or bleach in the water of the clear wash, or by putting the clear wash on cellophane before applying the watercolor paper over it.).

See the illustrations of Kathy M., Elise R., Hunter R., and Maria S. in the Heart Book pages, as well as Mary's here, as they used watercolor to illustrate the poems they chose for one of their double-page spreads.

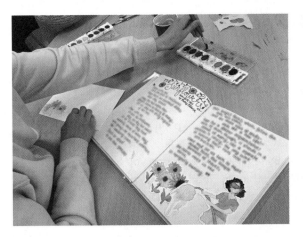

I recommend the following books (with beautiful watercolors):

> Adoff, Arnold. 1991. *In for Winter, Out for Spring*. New York: Harcourt Brace Jovanovich.
>
> Neruda, Pablo. 2003. *On the Blue Shore of Silence*. New York: HarperCollins.

I recommend the following for more extensive watercolor techniques:

> Johnson, Cathy. 1995. *Painting Watercolors*. Cincinnati, OH: North Light Books.
>
> Koliadych, Anna. 2019. *15-Minute Watercolor Masterpieces*. Salem, MA: Page Street Publishing.

Gift of Writing

The students save their leaf and shell watercolors in their writer's-reader's notebooks, or their portfolios, so they can use them in a few weeks. Since this is one of the first Art Invitations I ask them to try, it is the perfect opportunity to have them search through their notebooks for something they wrote that they might like to share with a parent, grandparent, friend, or anyone else during the holiday break. This is an option, not an assignment. They use the watercolor piece as the cover of their card. In the notes section of their writer's-reader's notebooks, they have written down the process for doing a wet-on-wet watercolor wash.

Cut or Torn Paper/Shapes and Designs

Cut or *torn paper* is one of the easier ideas for crafting an illustration, especially for the students who insist, "I am not an artist." Cutting the paper ensures smooth edges that blend or join together easily. Tearing the paper gives a texture to the edges and adds depth in the images or scenes the student is crafting.

To tear the paper, hold the image side up, or any side up if using plain paper. Keeping thumbs close together, tear one side of the paper away from you. The side torn from you will be rough, while the other side will be smooth. By reversing direction as you tear, away from you, then toward you, you create a rugged/smooth edge. Tearing the paper in different directions gives a ragged edge to it, which is effective as used for trees, mountains, waves—anything in nature that never has a straight edge.

Cutting the paper allows more specificity to the design. Both are easy and effective.

Planning for the illustration, and laying it out on the pages, whether an object or design, before writing the poem or response on the double-page spread, proves helpful to ensuring a proper and artistic fit.

Emma L. created an illustration for the Stanley Kunitz poem "End of Summer." She saw it as a rather sad poem, Kunitz describing what he saw as "part of my life" being "over." Emma tried to show the beauty of life slipping into the dark of the ocean, reflecting Kunitz's words, in her sunset. Even after she was done she said, "I was thinking I should have torn the edges, as life is not as smooth as this looks. It is rough."

Teaching the students to find the feeling in the poem and then thinking through the shapes and colors that might show that feeling helps them with an image. Or they might have first "seen" an image in the words of the poem that resonates with them, and then think through colors and shapes that reflect the feeling.

See the following student pages for more examples of cut or torn paper: Briana B., Hunter R., and Sophie W.

Additional Materials to Use as Examples for Cut or Torn Paper Images

Art postcards, especially those of:

Eric Carle, Wolf Kahn, Georgia O'Keeffe

Illustrations from:

Alexander, Kwame. 2017. *Out of Wonder*. With Chris Colderly and Marjory Wentworth. Somerville, MA: Candlewick Press.

Burrowes, Adjoa J. 2000. *Grandma's Purple Flowers*. New York: Lee & Low Books.

Miranda, Anne. 1993. *Night Songs*. New York: Bradbury Press.

All three books have wonderful illustrations that could be used as ideas for designs or making a collage.

Try This: Torn Paper

Materials

Give each student 5–7 pieces of 3 × 5-inch construction paper in different colors and a blank 5 × 8-inch index card.

Directions

Show students an example of a torn paper collage (see below) that took about three minutes to make. Notice the rough edges come from ripping the paper in different directions. Have students build a simple design or scene, glue pieces down, and put this Art Invitation: Torn Paper in their writer's-reader's notebook (I have my kids put it in the notes section.).

On the following double-page spread Jennifer shows us how to craft torn and cut paper into an appealing illustration, but she teaches us even more in her response to this poem. She chooses to personify loneliness, "the friend I've gotten too close to in the past year," and whose favorite flowers are lilies." Our students reveal their lives to us in many ways. Adolescence is so tough. Each time I talk to her I want to keep in mind her feelings of loneliness—the ache, the fear, the sadness she feels from this emptiness, and her wish to outrun it. It is real to her. I hear her. The illustration may not mean as much as her feelings and the way she connects to this poem, but they highlight something that does matter to her: lilies, the favorite flowers of her friend loneliness, and, perhaps, her favorite also.

"The Rider" by Naomi Shihab Nye

From Fuel (1998)

RESPONSE: I chose this poem because I relate strongly to the feeling of loneliness. (Though quite a different feeling than of being alone. Being alone is a choice, a deal, being content in the silence, while being lonely is a state of being. It's not a choice, just something put on you without any say from you at all. Wishing with all your heart that you could be anything but lonely.) Loneliness is a feeling I've gotten to get close to in the past year. I know her two middle names and how she got that scar on her arm. I know the color of her eyes: it's a mix of blue and grey and black, they scream at you like an angry ocean. I've gotten to know her favorite colors and how her favorite flowers are lilies. But I never chose lonely. I never wanted to feel an emptiness start to hole inside me. A black pit. Or this strange sensation of isolation, in a room full of people, with my own family. Or a sense of drowning and falling deeper and deeper in a ditch I dug myself. But sometimes it feels like, if I distract myself hard enough, I can outrun loneliness, outsmart the ache she brings me. How nice it would be if I could click my heels, transport myself to a world where I could have someone.

In this poem, I noticed Nye broke the lines in the middle of the sentences, like phrases in a sentence, where the reader could naturally pause and breathe. I like the verse "A boy once told me/If he roller-skated fast enough/his loneliness wouldn't catch up with him." I think that's really pretty, the way she phrased it. This poem means that familiar sense of loneliness to me. Of dread and fear and utter sadness. If only . . . (I could outrun it.)

In the words of Naomi Shihab Nye:
"It is really hard to be lonely very long in a world of words."

Collage

Collage comes from the French verb *coller*, meaning "to glue." It is an art technique in which various materials, such as paper, photos, fabric, pictures, writing, book pages, watercolor, are arranged by overlapping, joining, or blending to create a new image or a particular effect. The pieces are glued to a flat service.

In a second art lesson after students learn the wet-on-wet technique of watercolor, I show them several of the videos describing the use of salt, bleach, and plastic wrap with watercolor. (See the Art Invitation on contour drawing and watercolor for the YouTube videos on these techniques.) I then ask them to make two to three different pieces of watercolor paper using the techniques that interested them the most. I explain that we are going to let these papers dry, collect them, and have them available for any student's use when making a collage. This gives students lots of options for building a collage.

I also have on hand lots of construction paper, pieces of wrapping paper collected from samples used as a fundraiser for the school, old cards, magazine pages, book pages and covers from old books, photos, and so on.

I show examples from previous years—the ones I have collected and shared here. While many of these are cut from the various pieces of watercolor paper, others have included construction paper, drawing, and watercolor to add to the effect.

I constructed these last two collages so that I had something to show the students in addition to the collage work of professional artists. In the first one, I illustrated a poem about the city. I used construction paper and watercolor paper from the students' papers. In the second one, I made a photo collage illustrating Joyce Sutphen's poem "More of Everything," after seeing what my friend Penny Kittle did in her notebook with the same poem; I wanted to illustrate the line "the people who made me possible." I made a copy of a telegram my dad sent to my mom in 1943, asking when she would arrive in Johnson City, and saying how much he missed her. I found and copied pictures of my mom and dad and grandparents to build the collage. I kept the telegram central, focusing on the love of family that "made me possible."

I recommend the following books for collage illustrations:

Abiade, Folami, Dinah Johnson, Carole Boston Weatherford, Dakari Hur, et al. 1997. *In Daddy's Arms I Am Tall*. New York: Lee & Low Books.

Alexander, Kwame. 2017. *Out of Wonder*. With Chris Colderly and Marjory Wentworth. Somerville, MA: Candlewick Press.

Burrowes, Adjoa J. 2000. *Grandma's Purple Flowers*. New York: Lee & Low Books.

Carle, Eric. 1992. *Draw Me a Star*. New York: Philomel Books.

Miranda, Anne. 1993. *Night Songs*. New York: Bradbury Press.

Shange, Ntozake. 1994. *I Live in Music*. New York: St. Martin's Press.

All six books have wonderful illustrations that could be used as ideas for designs with torn or cut paper or for making a collage, especially using mixed media. One YouTube video that appears most helpful and extends the possibilities with collage is "How to Make a Collage—Materials, Composition, and Tips" posted by user Mr. Otter Art Studio on November 15, 2018.

Zentangles

A *Zentangle* is an abstract design that is deliberate and purposely structured (it is *not* a doodle), yet unexpected. (If you search for "Zentangles" online, hundreds of patterns and designs come up. These patterns are called "tangles." I usually "borrow" one of the simplest cluster of patterns and show the students many of the possibilities.)

Directions

1. Draw a border: With a pencil draw a light square border inside the edges of your paper. Press lightly with the pencil.
2. Draw a string or strings: A string is a curved line or random squiggle that shapes an area in which to draw the tangle. The pattern you create will emerge according to the contours of your string. It should be lightly sketched. The strings serve as a guide by giving structure to your pattern. Once you have done your design in pencil, go over the lines with a fine black pen and begin creating the tangles.
3. Start creating a tangle: A "tangle" is a pattern drawn in pen within the contours of a string. Keep the pattern consistent within each string.

A Zentangle can be drawn within any kind of design. You will notice that the examples I drew for students are marine organisms. Throughout the year I try to make as many connections with other disciplines as possible. At the end of the year our science teacher focuses on marine biology. Students choose an organism connected in any way to the ocean to study in depth. Although it may not be connected to their Heart Maps, I invite them to focus their last double-page spread of the year with the following instructions:

> Draw a rough outline of your marine biology organism—one you studied or any other found along the coast—inside the border of your paper. (See my outlines of the Sea Star and the Moon Snail.)
>
> Think about the contours and lines of your organism, and use patterns that follow those contour lines.
>
> Keep creating different patterns within each string until the design is complete.
>
> Find a poem that extends the meaning of the Zentangle and "sits well beside" your art. I recommend looking at Mary Oliver, Pablo Neruda, Lilian Moore, or Ogden Nash, although there are so many others who write about the sea, explicitly or metaphorically.
>
> You may also write your own poem.
>
> Explain the decisions you made while drawing your Zentangle and what you learned about the organism through study. Explain why you think the poem you chose sits well beside your Zentangle.
>
> Your Zentangle is the art work/illustration for your last double-page spread in your Heart Book.

Here are some examples from previous years:

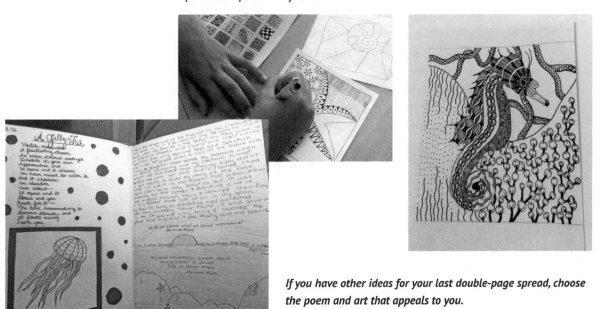

If you have other ideas for your last double-page spread, choose the poem and art that appeals to you.

About the Lionfish:

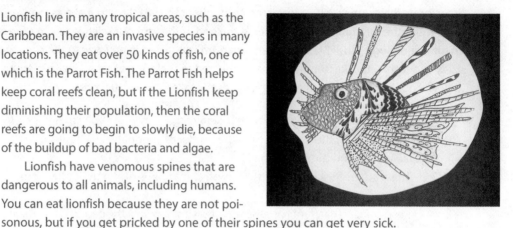

Lionfish live in many tropical areas, such as the Caribbean. They are an invasive species in many locations. They eat over 50 kinds of fish, one of which is the Parrot Fish. The Parrot Fish helps keep coral reefs clean, but if the Lionfish keep diminishing their population, then the coral reefs are going to begin to slowly die, because of the buildup of bad bacteria and algae.

Lionfish have venomous spines that are dangerous to all animals, including humans. You can eat lionfish because they are not poisonous, but if you get pricked by one of their spines you can get very sick.

The Lionfish hunts and catches its prey by sneaking up on it and cornering it with its large pectoral fins that can spread out to confuse its prey. Then the Lionfish lunges out and swallows its prey whole. It only uses its venomous spines for defense, not for hunting.

—Max T.

About the Zentangle:

For my zentangle, I drew the Lionfish. The first string of the Lionfish, where its eyes are located, is decorated with a pattern of scales to represent it being a scaled fish. I chose the pattern to the right of that one to be designed after coral, because of the Lionfish's effect on coral reefs. The last string to the right of the coral design just before its tail represents the actual stripes of the Lionfish, which has orange and white stripes in real life.

The design of the pectoral fins is dots and lines, the dots representing the venom inside of the spines, and the lines representing the stripes and lines of the physical attributes of the fish. Each of the spines on the top of the fish are related to designs on the fins and main body of the fish, the first representing the coral, the second representing venom.

—Max T.

Try This: Zentangle

On the web, search for "Zentangles" and print a sheet of designs that students can use as they practice the shapes. Give each student a 5 × 8-inch unlined index card. Use a simple shape like the one shown here, or let the students design any shape for practice. Each line or string defines an area for a different pattern or tangle. They can use Zentangles with any poem but they might want to match the shapes to the content. When my students had poems for marine organisms they used shapes like nets, clams, scales, or seaweed.

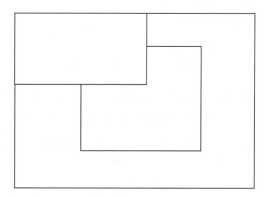

The sample can be put in the notes section of their writer's-reader's notebooks, or journals, if they have one. There are more examples of Zentangles in the Heart Book pages of Gwyneth, Aaron, Mia, and Maria.

Your students could use Zentangles as an illustration for any poems they are choosing.

Photography

Dorothea sees with her eyes *and* her heart. (Rosenstock 2016)

From the book jacket of Dorothea's *Eyes*, we learn that Dorothea Lange "used her photographs to tell the stories of the people the world ignored: the homeless, the jobless, the hungry, the poor" (2016). If there is anything we can try to teach our students through teaching them photography, it may be *compassion* and *gratitude*. Compassion for the people the world ignores. Gratitude for all that life offers us. It is worth the time to begin this art invitation by reading aloud *Dorothea's Eyes* to your students and having a short discussion of all she was trying to do with her photos.

You might then invite your students to try one of the following:

◆ Poem comes first: Take your own photo(s) or use professional photos to sit beside a poem that is meaningful to you.

◆ Photo comes first: Find a poem to sit beside a photo(s) (yours or those of a professional) that is meaningful to you. .

◆ Manipulate the photo of the poem in any way to further enhance your thinking from the poem and/or the photo.

In my writer's-reader's notebook I glued a photo of the spot where I sat with my computer each day for more than a year during the height of the pandemic. I realized I often simply sat at this window, staring out at the empty street that began to fill with walkers as the pandemic dragged on. I felt like I was losing words, with few people with whom to talk. I glued the photo into my notebook, over the words I was working too hard to find and thus meant little to me. I found a poem of hope about the good things that might come from the pandemic, but decided to cut them into strips to show how life had been pulled apart, and in my staring I wondered if we were all gazing at empty streets out windows that held the silences around us.

Ask your students to try this also—manipulate the layout of a poem with a photo to further enhance what they noticed about it and took to heart from it.

In his wonderful book *Focus Lessons*, Ralph Fletcher (2019) relates a conversation he had on a photo trip with Arthur Morris, a professional bird photographer and former New York City teacher:

> "It seems that getting strong pictures depends a lot on showing up," I said to him one day. "A lot of it hinges on being there, at the right place and time."
> Artie nodded. "Yes, lots of days you get up early and shoot pictures of stuff you've seen before. Occasionally you get a picture of something you've never seen before. And once in a great while, if you're lucky, you get a picture of something nobody has ever seen before. That's special." (7)

I believe, just as Ralph believes, that that is the same with writing. If you spend enough time putting words to paper, you may even think and say something in a way that nobody else has said it before.

"Try for that in your photos," I say to the students. "Try to capture something nobody has seen before. Try for that in your writing; try to say things in a way that nobody has said it like that before. Try that in your reading. Notice ways that writers phrase things, or use language, or punctuation, or layout on the page in ways you have never seen before. All take practice, practice, practice."

I am not so much about teaching a course in photography to students. In the limited time I have with them each day, and considering the fact we are working on the Heart Books only two to three days every six or eight weeks, I am more about giving them hints that are generally (but not always) true: move in close; make sure the light is behind you; use early morning and late afternoon light to create shadows; change your point of view (get on the ground if your subject is at ground level, or stand above the subject); find images that surprise you, stun you, calm you, shock you, sadden you, anger you (make you feel something!); color and light evoke feelings of calmness (dark colors) or energy (bright colors); put the main subject off-center to create interest; see with your eyes and your heart.

Like a good piece of writing, a good photograph is often about moving in close on the subject. And yet, when I put three photos together that move in closer, I like seeing the process of moving in and in and in. Each photo in this set of photos tells a story for me.

Phrases that come to mind include "favorite month October, when the air is green pear crisp"; "driving down Durham Point Road, roll down the window and breathe in the air as the trees take their last taste of summer: maples turning apple red, hickory summer squash yellow, oak pumpkin orange"; "as a kid in Hingham, raking leaves onto the side of Butler Road, where all the neighbors were also raking, burning, smiling, waving"; "the autumn of our lives drifting in to winter; cutting, splitting, stacking logs for the wood stove." So many directions in which I might go to sit one or more of these images beside a poem.

At Kylene and Brad Beers' ranch in Waco, Texas, there was so little rain and so much heat in the summer of 2018 that the pond surrounded by red cypress trees began to dry up. From the first photo one cannot see any problem. The second photo begins to tell the story—the roots are beginning to be exposed. The needles are turning yellow. Without water the trees, whose roots are so exposed in the third photo, will surely die. I begin to wonder about climate change and what we have done to cause this. It also gets me thinking about Naomi Shihab Nye's (2008) "Gate A-4" and the line, "an old country tradition. Always carry a plant. Always stay rooted to somewhere." My search begins for a poem that sits well beside one or all of these images.

In my Heart Book I used this photo of my dad to highlight the impact of war, especially on him. By cutting this photo into several strips, I meant to show how much he was "torn apart" by his experiences of being one member of the US armed forces that landed on the beaches of Normandy on D-Day during World War II. One survivor—who always wondered why he had not died there.

I had the poem or poems but wanted a picture to illustrate the trauma of war. With his arm around me as a toddler, wrapping me so fully, he is protecting me. I would never know the horrors of all he experienced until years later when his alcoholism and nightmares converge. Even then, I will only know a small piece of his experiences.

I want students to see they can change pictures to further enhance the feeling they are taking from, or taking to, a poem. It is intentional, meant to elaborate on the reader's thinking about the poem.

Iconic photos, such as the picture of Aylan Kurdi, the three-year-old Syrian refugee lying facedown and lifeless on a beach in Turkey, when the rubber boat he and his family were in capsized as they tried to flee to Greece in 2015, or the picture of Phan Thi Kim Phuc, a terrified nine-year-old Vietnamese girl, fleeing naked after being burned by a napalm bomb dropped by a South Vietnamese plane in 1972, carry more of an emotional impact and cause more concern for an issue than the statistical accounts of body counts.

Teaching students how to take photographs, as well as how to read them, carries importance well beyond the Heart Books. It may be in their discomfort, in their questions, in their shock and surprise that they discover new understandings about their world and the worlds of others. It may be through photos such as these, and those of other professional photographers like Dorothea Lange, that they develop compassion.

An especially moving spoken word poem about Aylan Kurdi was written and presented by Emi Mahmoud, a Sudanese American slam poet. Using Mahmoud's piece as a mentor text, students could produce a similar piece by taking a poem that is especially memorable for them or write their own based on a personal experience or a photograph, coupling it with images and music, and reading it aloud for a larger audience.

As a final evaluation/reflection of all they did and discovered about poetry and about themselves as they did the Heart Books, *what if* students had the option of crafting a video of the poem that meant the most to them, accompanied by a process paper of what they did as they did it, what problems they encountered, how they solved them, what they are most pleased with and what they would do differently in the next video? Penny Kittle and Kelly Gallagher's new book *4 Essential Studies* (2021) has a comprehensive section on Digital Composition. Showing the Mahmoud video a second time, and asking, "What do you notice she does?" would be a good way to begin.

I recommend the following resources:

Fletcher, Ralph. 2019. *Focus Lessons: How Photography Enhances the Teaching of Writing*. Portsmouth, NH: Heinemann.

> *In Appendix A of Ralph's book, he cites a number of sites online that are good resources for finding photographs for the classroom. I especially like:*
>
> *www.nytimes.com/column/learning-whats-going-on-in-this-picture and www.loc.gov/rr/print/coll/fbj/Every_Photo_home.html.*

Gaige, Amity. 1990. *We Are a Thunderstorm*. Kansas City, MI: Landmark Editions.

> *The poetry and photography of Amity Gaige as a sixteen-year-old.*

Kittle, Penny, and Kelly Gallagher. 2021. *4 Essential Studies*. Portsmouth, New Hampshire: Heinemann.

Mahmoud, Emi. 2016. "Boy in the Sand." https://www.unhcr.org/en-us/news /videos/2016/9/57cfe9fa4/boy-in-the-sand-by-emi-mahmoud.html.

> *A powerful spoken word poem crafted with images and music by Emi Mahmoud.*

Pakarklis, Emil (YouTube user iPhone Photography School). "7 Little-Known Tricks for Incredible iPhone Photography" posted on October 27, 2017, and "Secrets for Taking Incredible iPhone Reflection Photos" posted on May 26, 2017.

> *Both of Pakarklis's YouTube videos are short and clear, and give simple suggestions for taking unique photos with the iPhone camera, which most kids have. So easy to use in the classroom.*

Rosenstock, Barb. 2016. *Dorothea's Eyes*. Honesdale, PA: Calkins Creek.

Rylant, Cynthia. 1994. *Something Permanent*. Orlando, FL: Harcourt Brace.

> *The poetry of Cynthia Rylant in response to photographs by Walker Evans.*

Evaluation Form

POEM

Heart Book	#1	#2	#3	#4	#5
Poem title Poet Source Date completed spread					

Layout
    Appealing
    Easy to read
 	
Illustration
    Enhances poem					

Notice About poem Explanations Connections					

Poet's thoughts
 	
    On writing
 	
    On poetry
 	
    On reading
 	
    On . . .
 	
At least three quotes from the poet citing source/s used					

Comments:

A Note About Recommendations and References

I am not fond of labeling of any kind.

In my classroom I have always shied away from labeling books, whether by topic, issue, or big ideas, by writer as contemporary or classic (kids always thought that merely meant alive or dead), or by authors of color. Because I needed a way to organize books for ease in finding, I put them on the shelves alphabetically by last name of the author, with a different-color sticker based solely on genre. As I learn more about the students, from Day One, I make sure that the books I have allow each reader to see themselves and see the world in ways they may never have seen the world. If they can't, and don't, I need to find other books.

This is to explain why there is no list at the end of this book that says, "Recommended Authors of Color" or "Diverse Book List." Chad Everett (2017), a principal in Mississippi, says that "there are no diverse texts. It is in the transaction (Rosenblatt 1986) between the reader and the text that a text's diversity is realized." He goes on to cite Rudine Sims Bishop (1990), who emphasizes the need "for readers to have access to Mirror, Window, and Sliding-glass door texts. It is impossible to know which one of these roles a book will take on until it is in a reader's hands." For another reader, the book will take on a different role. "This is the beauty of good literature," Everett says, "it cannot be placed into one category or relegated to the 'diversity and inclusion' shelf."

Knowing your students and knowing authors (or poets) are what help you put books (or poems) in their hands.

RECOMMENDATIONS

Poetry as Video

Bryant, Kobe. "Dear Basketball." https://www.youtube.com/watch?v=bFVwNH3W_bA.

Dorfman, Andrea, filmmaker, with Tanya Davis, poet. "How to Be at Home." https://www.nfb.ca/film/how-to-be-at-home/.

Online Sites for Finding Poetry and Poets

American Life in Poetry. Kwame Dawes curator, formerly Ted Kooser. https://www.americanlifeinpoetry.org/.

Brainy Quotes. "Poetry Quotes." https://www.brainyquote.com/topics/poetry-quotes.

Library of Congress. Billy Collins. Poetry 180: A Poem a Day for American High Schools. https://www.loc.gov/programs/poetry-and-literature/poet-laureate/poet-laureate-projects/poetry-180/all-poems/.

Button Poetry

Keillor, Garrison: *The Writer's Almanac*. http://www.writersalmanac.org.

Nye, Naomi Shihab. https://www.poetryfoundation.org/video/series/154432/poetryevents. (Young People's Poet Laureate, N. S. Nye, reads poems and answers questions about poetry.)

Poem Hunter. https://www.poemhunter.com. (Search for poet's name and title of poem.)

Poets.org. https://www.poets.org.

Poetry Foundation. https://www.poetryfoundation.org/poets/pablo-neruda. (Search for poet's name at the poetry foundation—example here is Neruda.)

Poetry Out Loud. http://www.poetryoutloud.org.

Robert Pinsky's Favorite Poem Project. http://www.favoritepoem.org/thevideos/index.html. (Includes videos of poems being read with a bit of background on the reader.)

Teaching Living Poets. Find poets. https://teachlivingpoets.com/find-poets/.

Spoken Word Poets

(All are easily found on YouTube.)

Acevedo, Elizabeth. "Hair."

Anderson, Lemon. "Please Don't Take My Air Jordans."

Bournes, Micah: "Echoes of the Foremothers." https://micahbournes.bandcamp.com/album/echoes-of-the-foremothers (Reading Ntozake Shange's poem "My Father Is a Retired Magician.")

Gatwood, Olivia. "When I Say That We Are All Teen Girls."

Goodwin, Idris. "Say My Name."

Gorman, Amanda (nation's first Youth Poet Laureate). "The Hill We Climb."

Kay, Sarah. "Hands."

———. "If I Should Have a Daughter."

———. "Montauk."

———. "Point-B."

Mojgani, Anis. "Shake the Dust."

Prince EA. "Everybody Dies, But Not Everybody Lives."

Smith, Ethan. "A Letter to the Girl I Used to Be."

Yamazawa, G. "Elementary."

Novels in Verse

(These are either books my students recommended or books I would use if I were still in the classroom.)

Acevedo, Elizabeth. 2018. *The Poet X*. New York: HarperCollins.

———. 2020. *Clap When You Land*. New York: Harper Teen.

Alexander, Kwame. 2014. *The Crossover*. New York: Houghton Mifflin Harcourt.

———. 2016. *Booked*. New York: Houghton Mifflin Harcourt.

———. 2017. *Solo*. New York: HarperCollins.

———. 2018a. *Rebound*. New York: Houghton Mifflin Harcourt.

———. 2018b. *Swing*. New York: HarperCollins.

Anderson, Laura Halse. 2019. *Shout*. New York: Viking Penguin Random House.

Browne, Mahogany. 2021. *Chlorine Sky*. New York: Random House.

Creech, Sharon. 2001. *Love That Dog*. New York: HarperCollins.

Farish, Terry. 2012. *The Good Braider*. Tarrytown, New York: Marshall Cavendish.

Grimes, Nikki. 2002. *Bronx Masquerade*. New York: Penguin Group.

Hesse, Karen. 1997. *Out of the Dust*. New York: Scholastic.

———. 2001. *Witness*. New York: Scholastic.

Kearney, Meg. 2005. *The Secret of Me*. New York: Persea Books.

———. 2012. *The Girl in the Mirror*. New York: Persea Books.

———. 2017. *When You Never Said Goodbye*. New York: Persea Books.

Lai, Thanhha. 2011. *Inside Out & Back Again*. New York: HarperCollins.

Reynolds, Jason. 2017. *Long Way Down*. New York: Simon and Schuster.

Salazar, Aida. 2020. *Land of the Cranes*. New York: Scholastic.

Turner, Ann. 2000. *Learning to Swim*. New York: Scholastic.

Warga, Jasmine. 2019. *Other Words for Home*. New York: HarperCollins.

Woodson, Jacqueline. 2014. *Brown Girl Dreaming*. New York: Penguin Group.

Sports Poetry

Alexander, Kwame. (See his books under "Novels in Verse.")

Blaustein, Noah. 2001. *Motion: American Sports Poems*. Iowa City, IA: University of Iowa Press.

Knudson, R. R., and May Swenson. 1995. *American Sports Poems*. New York: Orchard Books.

Miller, E. Ethelbert. 2018. *If God Invented Baseball: Poems*. Westport, CT: City Point.

Morrison, Lillian, comp. 1995. *Slam Dunk*. New York: Hyperion Books.

Eight Random Books I Highly Recommend

Alexander, Kwame, with Chris Colderley and Marjory Wentworth. 2017. *Out of Wonder*. Somerville, MA: Candlewick.

Bosak, Susan V. 2004. *Dream*. Whitchurch-Stouffville, Ontario: TCP.

Crews, James, ed. 2021. *How to Love the World*. North Adams, MA: Storey.

Intrator, Sam M., and Megan Scribner, eds. 2003. *Teaching with Fire*. San Francisco, CA: Jossey-Bass.

Paschen, Elise. 2010. *Poetry Speaks: Who I Am*. Illinois: Sourcebooks Jabberwocky.

Quinn, Alice, ed. 2020. *Together in a Sudden Strangeness: America's Poets Respond to the Pandemic*. New York: Alfred A. Knopf.

Stafford, Kim. 2021. *Singer Come from Afar*. Pasadena, CA: Red Hen.

Whitney, Diana, ed. 2021. *You Don't Have to Be Everything: Poems for Girls Becoming Themselves*. New York: Workman.

REFERENCES

(For the ease of teachers' use, I have separated books and other resources that are particularly useful for teaching the Art Invitations and listed them with the respective art technique, including references for "Why Art in the English/Language Arts Classroom?")

Abeel, Samantha. 1994. *Reach for the Moon*. Duluth, MN: Pfeifer-Hamilton.

Acevedo, Elizabeth. 2018. *The Poet X*. New York: HarperCollins.

Adoff, Arnold. 1991. *In for Winter, Out for Spring*. Orlando, FL: Harcourt Brace Jovanovich.

Albers, Peggy. 2007. *Finding the Artist Within*. Newark, DE: International Reading Assoc.

Alexander, Kwame. 2007. *Crush*. Alexandria, VA: Word of Mouth Books.

——. 2012. *And Then You Know*. Alexandria, VA: Word of Mouth Books.

Angelou, Maya. 2003. *Just Give Me a Cool Drink of Water 'fore I Diiie*. UK: Time Warner Books.

Appelt, Kathi. 2002. *Poems from Homeroom*. New York: Henry Holt.

Aronson, Sarah. 2018. "'Poetry in America' with PBS Host and Creator Elisa New." Montana Public Radio. November 8.

Atwell, Nancie. 2006. *Naming the World*. Portsmouth, NH: Heinemann.

Baca, Jimmy Santiago. 2011. *Selected Poems of Jimmy Santiago Baca*. New York: A New Directions Book.

Bagert, Brod, ed. 1995. *Poetry for Young People: Edgar Allen Poe*. New York: Sterling.

Baker, David. n.d. "The Sea." https://poets.org>poem>O.

Becker, Abigail Lynne. 1993. *A Box of Rain*. South Berwick, ME: self-published by Linda Becker.

Beers, Kylene. 1987. *Reading Strategies Handbook for High School*. New York: Holt, Rinehart and Winston.

Bishop, Rudine Sims. 1990. "Mirrors, Windows, and Sliding Glass Doors." *Perspectives: Choosing and Using Books for the Classroom* 6 (3).

Blaustein, Noah, Ed. 2001. *Motion: American Sports Poems*. Iowa City, IA: University of Iowa Press.

Bolin, Frances Schoonmaker, ed. 1994. *Poetry for Young People: Emily Dickinson*. New York: Sterling.

——. 1995. *Poetry for Young People: Carl Sandburg*. New York: Sterling.

Bruchac, Joseph, and Jonathan London. 1992. *Thirteen Moons on Turtle's Back*. New York: Philomel Books.

Bryan, Ashley. 1992. *Sing to the Sun*. New York: HarperCollins.

Bunchman, Janis. 1994. *Pictures & Poetry*. Worcester, MA: Davis Publications.

Burrowes, Adjoa J. 2000. *Grandma's Purple Flowers*. New York: Lee & Low Books.

Carlisle, Andrea. 2010. "Emily Dickinson's To-Do List." *The Writer's Almanac*. December 10.

Christie, Michael. 2015. "All Parents Are Cowards." *New York Times*. February 15.

Clark, Amy. 2017. "No More Apologies." *Sometimes You Just Need a Poem* (blog), August 30. http://sometimesyoujustneedapoem.wordpress.com/2017/08/30/no-more-apologies/.

Clark, Colleen Patrice. 2016. "Literature's Empowerment." *Literacy Today* (March/April).

Cooper, Wyn, 2018. *Mars Poetica*. VT: White Pine Press.

Cummings, Pat. 1992. *Talking with Artists*. Vol. 1. New York: Bradbury Press.

De Fina, Allan A. 1997. *When a City Leans Against the Sky*. Honesdale, PA: Boyds Mills Press.

Dellamaggiore, Katie, director. 2012. *Brooklyn Castle* (documentary film).

Dickinson, Emily. 1994. *The Selected Poems of Emily Dickinson*. Hertfordshire, England: Wordsworth Poetry Library.

Doran, Joel. n.d. "Horseshoe Crab." PoemHunter.com.

Doty, Mark. 2010. "Tide of Voices: Why Poetry Matters Now." August 8. https://poets.org /text/tide-voices-why-poetry-matters-now.

Dunning, Stephen, Edward Lueders, and Hugh Smith, eds. 1966. *Reflections of a Gift of Watermelon Pickle*. New York: Scott, Foresman.

Elliott, Zetta. 2020. *Say Her Name*. New York: Disney—Jump at the Sun.

Everett, Chad. 2017. "There Is No Diverse Book." *ImagineLIT* (blog). November 21.

Farrell, Kate. 1995. *Art and Nature*. New York: Little, Brown.

Feelings, Tom. 1993. *Soul Looks Back in Wonder*. New York: Dial Books.

Fletcher, Ralph. 1997. *Ordinary Things*. New York: Atheneum Books.

———. 2001. *Have You Been to the Beach Lately?* New York: Orchard.

———. 2003. *Hello, Harvest Moon*. New York: Houghton Mifflin.

Franck, Frederick. 1973. *The Zen of Seeing*. New York: Vintage.

Frost, Robert. 1935. Address. Milton, MA: Milton Academy. May 17.

———. 1975. *You Come Too*. New York: Henry Holt.

———. 1982. *A Swinger of Birches*. Owing Mills, MD: Stemmer House.

Frye, Mary Elizabeth. n.d. "Do Not Stand at My Grave and Weep." https:// Yourdailypoem .com/listpoem.jsp?poem_id=322.

Gaige, Amity. 1990. *We Are a Thunderstorm*. Kansas City, MO: Landmark Editions.

Giovanni, Nikki. 2002. *Quilting the Black-Eyed Pea*. New York: HarperCollins.

———. 2006. Poemhunter.com.

———. 2020. *Make Me Rain*. New York: HarperCollins.

Glass, Julia. 2002. *Three Junes*. New York: Anchor Books.

Gorman, Amanda. 2021. *The Hill We Climb: An Inaugural Poem for the Country*. New York: Viking.

Grimes, Nikki. 2017. *One Last Word*. New York: Bloomsbury Children's Books.

Hall, Donald. 1990. *Old and New Poems*. New York: Ticknor and Fields.

Harjo, Joy. 2019. *An American Sunrise*. New York: W. W. Norton.

Heaney, Seamus. 1988. *Poems 1965–1975*. New York: Farrar, Straus and Giroux.

Heard, Georgia. 1999. *Awakening the Heart: Exploring Poetry in Elementary and Middle School*. Portsmouth, NH: Heinemann.

———. 2016. *Heart Maps: Helping Students Create and Craft Authentic Writing*. Portsmouth, NH: Heinemann.

———. Ted Talk. https://www.google.com/search?q=Georgia+Heard+TedTalk&oq=Georgia
+Heard+TedTalk&aqs=chrome..69i57j0i22i30.8515j0j7&sourceid=chrome&ie=UTF-8.

Herrera, Juan Felipe. 2008. "Let Me Tell You What a Poem Brings." In *Half of the World in Light*. Tucson, AZ: University of Arizona Press.

Hinton, S. E. 1967. *The Outsiders*. New York: Viking Press.

Holbrook, Sara, and Allan Wolf. 2008. *More Than Friends: Poems from Him and Her*. Honesdale, PA: Wordsong.

Housden, Roger. 2018. *Ten Poems for Difficult Times*. Novato, CA: New World Library.

Hudson, Wade, and Cheryl Willis Hudson, eds. 2018. *We Rise, We Resist, We Raise Our Voices*. New York: Penguin Random House.

Intrator, Sam M., and Megan Scribner, eds. 2007. *Leading from Within*. San Francisco, CA: Jossey-Bass.

Irving, Washington. Fishing quotes. https://www.pinterest.com.

Janeczko, Paul B. 1983. *Poetspeak*. New York: Bradbury Press.

———. 1984. *Strings: A Gathering of Family Poems*. New York: Bradbury Press.

———. 2011. *Reading Poetry in the Middle Grades*. Portsmouth, NH: Heinemann.

Kaufman, Caroline. 2018. *Light Filters In*. New York: HarperCollins.

Kaur, Rupi. 2015. *Milk and Honey*. Kansas City, MO: Andrews McMeel.

———. 2017. *The Sun and Her Flowers*. Kansas City, MO: Andrews McMeel.

Keillor, Garrison. 2011. *Good Poems, American Places*. New York: Penguin Group.

Kingsolver, Barbara. 1998. *Another America*. New York: Seal Press.

Knudson, R. R., and May Swenson. 1995. *American Sports Poems*. New York: Orchard Books.

Kooser, Ted. 1985. *Flying at Night*. Pittsburgh, PA: University of Pittsburgh Press.

Kouyoumdjian, Haig. 2012. "Learning Through Visuals: Visual Imagery in the Classroom." *Get Psyched!* (blog). *Pyschology Today*, July 20.

Lacey, Marc. 2020. "How Poetry Shakes Up the National Desk's Morning Meetings." *New York Times*. March 5.

Lasky, Dorothea. 2012. "What Poetry Teaches Us About the Power of Persuasion," *The Atlantic*, October 13. http://www.theatlantic.com/national/archive/2012/10/what-poetry-teaches-us-about-the-power-of-persuasion/263551/.

Lathem, Edward Connery, ed. 1967. *The Poetry of Robert Frost*. New York: Holt Rinehart and Winston.

Lee, Min Jin. 2017. *Pachinko*. New York: Grand Central.

Lyon, George Ella. 1999. *Where I'm From*. Spring, TX: Absey.

———. 2013. *Many-Storied House*. Lexington, KY: The University Press of Kentucky.

MacGowan, Christopher, ed. 2004. *Poetry for Young People: William Carlos Williams*. New York: Sterling.

Marshak, Suzanna. 1991. *I Am the Ocean*. New York: Little, Brown.

McCullough, David. 1999. "David McCullough, the Art of Biography No. 2." Interviewed by Elizabeth Gaffney and Benjamin Ryder Howe. *The Paris Review* (Fall).

McIntyre, James. n.d. "Fight of a Buffalo with Wolves." https:// Poeticous.com/james-mcintyre/fight-of-a-buffalo-with-wolves.

Medina, Tony. 2002. *Love to Langston*. New York: Lee and Lothrop Books.

Meinke, Peter. 2012. *The Shape of Poetry*. Tampa, FL: The University of Tampa Press.

Mendelson, Edward, and Eric Copeland, eds. 2008. *Poetry for Young People: Lewis Carroll*. New York: Sterling.

Merwin, W. S. 1977. *The Compass Flower: Poems*. Boston, MA: Macmillan.

Miranda, Anne. 1993. *Night Songs*. New York: Bradbury.

Montilla, Yesenia. 2015. *The Pink Box*. Detroit, MI: Aquarius Press.

Nash, Ogden. 1997. *Under Water with Ogden Nash*. New York: Little, Brown.

Nelson, Marilyn. 2001. *Carver: A Life in Poems*. Asheville, NC: Front Street.

Neruda, Pablo. 2003. *The Poetry of Pablo Neruda*. New York: Farrar, Straus and Giroux.

———. 2004. *The Essential Neruda: Selected Poems*. San Francisco, CA: City Lights Books.

———. n.d. "If You Forget Me." https://Allpoetry.com/If-You-Forget-Me.

Nye, Naomi Shihab. 1992. *This Same Sky*. New York: Four Winds.

———. 1994. *Red Suitcase*. Rochester, New York: BOA Editions.

———. 1998. *Fuel*. Rochester, New York: BOA Editions.

———. 2005. *A Maze Me*. New York: HarperCollins.

———. 2008. *Honeybee*. New York: HarperCollins.

Oliver, Mary. 1992. *New and Selected Poems*. Boston, MA: Beacon.

———. 2004. *Blue Iris*. Boston, MA: Beacon.

———. 2008. *Red Bird*. Boston, MA: Beacon.

Owens, Delia. 2018. *Where the Crawdads Sing*. New York: G. P. Putnam's Sons.

Pan, Emily X. R. 2018. *The Astonishing Color of After*. New York: Little, Brown.

Piercy, Marge. 1980. *The Moon Is Always Female*. New York: Alfred A. Knopf.

———. 1992. *Mars and Her Children*. New York: Alfred A. Knopf.

Popova, Maria. 2019. "Planting Trees as Resistance and Empowerment: The Remarkable Illustrated Story of Wangari Maathai, the First African Woman to Win the Nobel Peace Prize." *The Marginalian*. https://www.brainpickings.org/2019/06/04/wangari-maathai -the-woman-who-planted-millions-of-trees/?mc_cid=e965f9da61&mc_eid=55b26d60e0.

———. 2020. "The Universe in Verse." *The Marginalian* (April).

Pourquié, Bernadette and Cécile Gambini. 2016. *Strange Trees and the Story Behind Them*. New York: Princeton Architectural Press.

Prelutsky, Jack. 1990. *Something Big Has Been Here*. New York: Greenwillow Books.

Prevot, Franck. 2015. *Wangari Maathai: The Woman Who Planted Millions of Trees*. Watertown, MA: Charlesbridge.

Prinselaar, Roberto J. n.d. "Korean War." (The poem is etched in stone at a Korean War Veterans' Memorial in the Liberty State Park NJ Turnpike.) http://generalmacarthurshonorguard.com/wordpress/the-stories/the-stories-korean-war-poem.

Reid, Alastair, transl. 2003. *Neruda: On the Blue Shore of Silence*. New York: HarperCollins.

Reynolds, Jason. 2016. *Ghost*. New York: Atheneum.

Rief, Linda. 2018. *The Quickwrite Handbook: 100 Mentor Texts to Jumpstart Your Students' Thinking and Writing*. Portsmouth, NH: Heinemann.

Rosenblatt, Louise M. 1986. *Literature as Exploration*. New York: Modern Language Association.

Ryan, Pam Muñoz. 2010. *The Dreamer*. New York: Scholastic.

Schmidt, Gary D., ed. 1994. *Poetry for Young People: Robert Frost*. New York: Sterling.

Schoonmaker, Frances, ed. 1998. *Poetry for Young People: Henry Wadsworth Longfellow*. New York: Sterling.

———. 1999. *Poetry for Young People: Edna St. Vincent Millay*. New York: Sterling.

Shakur, Tupac. 1999. *The Rose That Grew from Concrete*. New York: Pocket Books.

Shange, Ntozake. 1994. *I Live in Music*. New York: St. Martin's Press.

Sidman, Joyce. 2010. *Ubiquitous: Celebrating Nature's Survivors*. Boston, MA: Houghton Mifflin.

Siebert, Diane. 1991. *Sierra*. New York: HarperCollins.

Silverstein, Shel. 1974. *Where the Sidewalk Ends*. New York: HarperCollins.

———. 1981. *A Light in the Attic*. New York: Harper and Row.

———. 2011. *Every Thing on It*. New York: HarperCollins.

Simic, Charles. 2008. *That Little Something*. Orlando, FL: Houghton Mifflin Harcourt.

Sin, r.h. 2016. *Whiskey Words & a Shovel II*. Kansas City, MO: McMeel.

Smith, Clint. 2016. *Counting Descent*. Los Angeles, CA: Write Bloody.

Smith, Michael, and Jeffrey Wilhelm. 2002. *Reading Don't Fix No Chevys*. Portsmouth, NH: Heinemann.

Soto, Gary. 1990. *Who Will Know Us?* San Francisco, CA: Chronicle Books.

Stafford, William. 1994. *Learning to Live in the World*. Orlando, FL: Harcourt Brace.

———. 1998. *The Way It Is*. Saint Paul, MN: Graywolf Press.

Sutphen, Joyce. 2019. *Carrying Water to the Field: New and Selected Poems*. Lincoln, NE: University of Nebraska Press.

Taylor, A. P. 2015. "Pink Flamingo." https://hellopoetry.com.

VanDerwater, Amy Ludwig. 2018. *Poems Are Teachers*. Portsmouth, NH: Heinemann.

Walker, Alice. 1982. *The Color Purple*. New York: Penguin Books.

———. n.d. "When You See Water." http:// Poeticous.com/alice-walker /when-you-see-water.

West, Kathleen. 2008. "Deer Hunting Time Is Here Again." https://www .poemhunter.com/poem/deer-hunting-time-is-here-again/.

Wilbur, Richard. 1988. *New and Collected Poems*. San Diego, CA: Harcourt Brace Jovanovich.

Wiley, Rachel. 2017. *Nothing Is Okay*. Minneapolis, MN: Button Press.

Winnie-the-Pooh.pinterest.com.

Wood, Nancy. 1974. *Many Winters*. New York: Doubleday.

———. 1993. *Spirit Walker*. New York: Delacorte.

———. 1995. *Dancing Moons*. New York: Delacorte.

Woodson, Jacqueline. 2003. *Locomotion*. New York: Penguin Random House.

———. 2014. *Brown Girl Dreaming*. New York: Penguin Group.

———. 2020. *Before the Ever After*. New York: Penguin Random House.

Yeats, William Butler. n.d. "He Wishes for the Cloths of Heaven." https:// Scottishpoetrylibrary.org.uk/poem/he-wishes-cloths-heaven/.

ACKNOWLEDGMENTS

Several years ago, I presented at a four-day writing retreat sponsored by Heinemann in Boothbay Harbor, Maine, where Naomi Shihab Nye was our writer in residence. One evening after dinner a number of us, including Naomi and her mom, were sitting around the firepit on the deck of the inn, relaxing and talking after a day of presentations, writing, and deep thinking that had energized and inspired us. Someone said, "Naomi, would you be willing to read a few of your poems to us?" *Of course*, she would!

Picture this. Clear night. Ocean breeze. Moon and stars popping against the navy sky. Lobster boats gently heaving and lolling on their moorings. Atlantic Ocean rolling with waves cresting and breaking on the rocky shore. A fire crackling. The smell of sea salt, pine trees, and wood smoke. And Naomi Shihab Nye reading her poetry aloud.

As she was reading, a family came out of the restaurant and started down the steps to the separate cottages. A little boy, about nine years old, stopped on the steps. When his mom motioned him to follow, he whispered, politely, but loud enough for all of us to hear, "Can't we listen? I want to listen." They sat on the top step, joining us as we all relished the opportunity to listen to Naomi Shihab Nye.

This is what Naomi has given us—the opportunity to listen. Through poetry she shares the world in ways so many of us seldom see it. She makes us "want to listen." My shelves are filled with Naomi's books, which offer her heart and soul, her laughter and tears, her humanity—in ways no other poet has done to make me love poetry and want my eighth graders to love poetry.

Many other poets have been integral to this poetic journey for me: Georgia Heard, Roland Flint, Elizabeth Kirschner, Meg Kearney, Ralph Fletcher, Kwame Alexander. I am also inspired by teacher colleagues/friends whose reading and writing of poetry influence me daily: Penny Kittle, Tom Romano, Maureen Barbieri, Tomasen Carey, and Cathleen Greenwood.

Thanks especially to Georgia Heard for her poetry, for her Heart Maps, for her generosity, her humility, and her kindness in her very being. These Heart Books came to be under so much of her work and influence.

Karen Ernst helped me see the value in art as it sits beside and works with writing. Contour drawing. Move the pen. Look closely at your students. Practice. Practice. Practice. She made me stop saying "I can't draw" by doing it again and again and again—until I realized those sketches and drawings actually made me pay attention to the world around me, one student at a time. Tomasen Carey helped extend my thinking about the visual arts into photography, in a course that showed me how to move the camera in differently on an image, the same way one might do in writing. Change perspective. Notice from all angles.

Thank you to my eighth graders, who dove wholeheartedly into their Heart Books, and changed their minds about poetry, once they realized it wasn't what they always thought it was: "dumb, . . . girlie, . . . a waste of time." I miss all of you.

To the many Heinemann folks who worked through Covid while moving the Heinemann office: Roderick Spelman, Louisa Irele, Catrina Swasey, Sarah Fournier, Patty Adams, Josh Evans, and Suzanne Heiser, thank you for giving this book such attention and care.

Adapted from *Leading from Within: Poetry That Sustains the Courage to Lead* by Sam M. Intrator and Megan Scribner. Copyright © 2007 by the Center for Courage and Renewal. Reproduced with permission of John Wiley & Sons Limited through PLSclear.

AdaptedUMI from Awakening the Heart: Exploring Poetry in Elementary and Middle School by Georgia Heard. Copyright © 1999 by Georgia Heard. Published by Heinemann, Portsmouth, NH. Reprinted by permission of the Publisher. All rights reserved.

"Awkward Poems" from *Crush* by Kwame Alexander. Published 2007 by Word of Mouth Books. Reprinted by permission the author.

Poetry selection titled: "Mercury" from *Light Filters In: Poems* by Carline Kaufman, Illustrated By: Yelena Bryksenkova. Copyright © by Caroline Kaufman. Reprinted by permission of HarperCollins Publishers.

Poetry selection titled: "I Am Tired of Being Little" from *Something Big Has Been Here* by Jack Prelustsky. Illustrated by James Stevenson. Text copyright © 1990 by Jack Prelutsky. Illustrations copyright © by James Stevenson. Used by permission of HarperCollins Publishers.

"Simple Requests" from *We Are a Thunderstorm* by Amity Gaige. Copyright © 1990 by Amity Gaige. Reprinted by permission of InkWell Management on behalf of the author.

"Daffodils" from *Ordinary Things: Poems from a Walk in Early Spring* by Ralph Fletcher. Text copyright © 1997 by Ralph Fletcher. Reprinted by permission of the author.

"Sunset" from *Have You Been to the Beach Lately?: Poems* by Ralph Fletcher. Text copyright © 2001 by Ralph Fletcher. Reprinted by permission of the author.

"Shyness" from *Isla Negra* by Pablo Neruda, translated by Alastair Reid. Translation copyright © 1981 by Alastair Reid. Reprinted by permission of Farrar, Straus and Giroux. All rights reserved.

"Timidez" from *Memorial de Isla Negra* by Pablo Neruda. Copyright © 1964 by Pablo Neruda and the Fundación Pablo Neruda. Reprinted by permission of Agencia Literaria Carmen Balcells.

"What Would I Do…" by Abigail Becker from *A Box of Rain: A Collection of Writings*. Waters Lithograph, Inc., Wilmington, Mass. Copyright © 1995.

"Mars Poetica" from *Mars Poetica* by Wyn Cooper. Published 2018 by White Pine Press. Reprinted by permission of White Pine Press.

"Emily Dickinson's To-Do List" is reprinted by permission of the author, Andrea Carlisle, who owns the copyright for this poem. <Do we have a year or any other info for this?>

Numbered list from "The Visual-Verbal Connections of Literacy: An Examination of the Composing processes of the Fifth- and Sixth-Grade Student" by Kay Cowan. Unpublished doctoral dissertation, Georgia State University, 2001. Reprinted by permission of Kay Cowan.

About the Author

Linda Rief left the classroom in June of 2019 after 40 years of teaching Language Arts, mostly with eighth graders. She misses their energy and their apathy, their curiosity and their complacency, their confidence and their insecurities, but mostly she misses their passionate, powerful voices as readers and writers.

She is an instructor in the University of New Hampshire's Summer Literacy Institute and a national and international presenter on issues of adolescent literacy. She is the author of *The Quickwrite Handbook, Read Write Teach, Inside the Writer's-Reader's Notebook* and *Seeking Diversity;* she is co-editor (Beers, Probst, and Rief) of *Adolescent Literacy.*

In 2021 she was honored with the Distinguished Service Award from the National Council of Teachers of English. In 2020 she received the Kent Williamson Exemplary Leader Award from the Conference on English Leadership, in recognition of outstanding leadership in the English Language Arts. Her classroom was featured in the series *Making Meaning in Literature* produced by Maryland Public Television for Annenberg/CPB. For three years she chaired the first Early Adolescence English/Language Arts Standards Committee of the National Board for Professional Teaching Standards.

Her inspiration: granddaughters Julia and Fiona, and grandsons Hunter and Harrison